Interpreting Our Heritage

Interpreting Our Heritage

Third Edition

By
FREEMAN TILDEN

THE UNIVERSITY OF NORTH CAROLINA PRESS
CHAPEL HILL

© 1957, 1967, 1977 The University of North Carolina Press
All rights reserved
Manufactured in the United States of America
ISBN 0-8078-4016-5
Library of Congress Catalog Number 67-27763

98   97   96   95   94   20   19   18   17   16

Contents

PART ONE

PART TWO

vi CONTENTS

Illustrations

Between pages 60 and 61

Between pages 70 and 71

Between pages 80 and 81

Between pages 86 and 87

Between pages 96 and 97

Foreword to the Third Edition

FORMER Director of the National Park Service, Newton B. Drury, once observed that national parks are set aside not solely to preserve scenic landscapes and historic places. Parks provide a greater dividend because of their unique value in "mininstering to the human mind and spirit." In these perplexing times when more and more Americans seek to find in the parks leisure time alternatives to their everyday world, I believe this purpose and value is ever more significant.

A guiding hand is often helpful to realize this purpose, and millions of park visitors over the years have needed help to translate that which is perceived into that which relates personally to them as individuals and to bring into focus the truths that lie beyond what the eye sees. The guiding hand is the park interpreter, and it was to this professional communicator of environmental awareness and understanding that Freeman Tilden addressed his concepts nearly a generation ago with the first edition of *Interpreting Our Heritage*.

If this had been a book merely about the gadgetry and methodology of interpretation, it long ago would have been obsolete. But Freeman Tilden wrote about fundamentals—the guiding principles and underlying philosophy of the interpreter's art and craft. As pioneer of interpretive philosophy and recognized father of modern park interpretation, Tilden, through *Interpreting Our Heritage*, has made a profound mark on the park conservation movement in America.

It is no wonder that *Interpreting Our Heritage* has become an accepted classic in the literature of park management, read and reread by student and practitioner. His message remains as fresh as ever.

Sigurd Olson, a contemporary of Tilden, wrote, "While we are born with curiosity and wonder and our early years full of the adventure they bring, I know such inherent joys are often lost. I also know that, being deep within us, their latent glow can be fanned to flame again by awareness and an open mind."

In this volume Freeman Tilden teaches us how to fan that flame in the minds of others. With eloquent wit and wry humor he leads us to the "priceless ingredient": love of beauty in all its forms. His chapter on "The Happy Amateur" speaks for all people in their quest for enriching leisure time pursuits.

Park Service people have long considered Freeman a valued friend and associate, and it is a source of great pride that the National Park Service has collaborated with the author and publisher in all three editions of this book. I am personally delighted that Freeman Tilden's words will continue to endure as inspiration and counsel to all who are concerned with the stewardship of our nation's natural and cultural heritage.

GARY EVERHARDT
Director
National Park Service

Washington, D.C.
July, 1976

Foreword to the Second Edition

ANATOLE France said, "Do not try to satisfy your vanity by teaching a great many things. Awaken people's curiosity. It is enough to open minds; do not overload them. Put there just a spark. If there is some good inflammable stuff, it will catch fire.

To excite curiosity, to open a person's mind—there is challenge for anyone who seeks to communicate ideas. I know of no one more sensitive to the challenge than the interpreter, for he is a teacher in the purest sense of the word. He works with people who are at leisure, at the special places of beauty and history which have been dedicated and set aside. He seeks to translate, vividly, the language of the earth, and of the earth's inhabitants.

We consider interpretation to be one of the most important single activities of the National Park Service. And we are particularly proud of the contribution that the Service has made to the historical development of interpretation in this country, nurturing the seeds that the C. M. Goethes carried from Lake Lucerne to Lake Tahoe and thence to Yosemite in 1920. Here was a new learning experience for Americans—one that was pressure-free to take or leave, in surroundings of inspiration. For that very reason it could hardly fail. Today the interpreters in federal, state, and municipal parks and historic sites—whether archeologists, naturalists, historians—are direct descendants of these first nature guides.

Every year more people prove the validity of Frederick Law Olmsted's observation, made in 1865: "It is a scientific fact that the occasional contemplation of natural scenes of an impressive character, particularly if this contemplation occurs in connection with relief from ordinary cares, change of air and change of habits, is favorable to the health and vigor of men and especially to the health and vigor of their intellect beyond any other conditions which can be offered them, but it not only gives pleasure for the time being but increases the subsequent capacity for happiness and the means of securing happiness."

Interpreting Our Heritage has in the past decade become a basic guide in the field, and a textbook for college instruction in park management. The broad implications of interpretation to the field of education are effectively discussed in the introduction by Dr. Christopher Crittenden.

It is fortunate that the Old Dominion Foundation, established by Mr. Paul Mellon, provided a generous grant to the National Park Service to make possible the study of which this book, now in its second edition, is the end product. The debt of gratitude we owe to the Old Dominion Foundation wil be multiplied many times as other organizations benefit from it.

Since an objective of any park administration is to improve the quality of park use, the effectiveness of our interpretive program is a major concern of all administrators. Until the first edition of this book appeared in 1957, no one had attempted to analyze this fascinating new discipline, nor to identify its guiding principles. We are delighted that the demand for this volume has resulted in a revised edition.

No one is better equipped to communicate the elusive substance of the theory we call interpretation than Freeman Tilden. He has the unique ability to place before you the interpretive cake—its layers representing scope of interpretation, from his six basic principles to his final new chapter, "Vistas of Beauty," which describes a kind of metaphysical understanding that can be transmitted from interpreter to visitor. This understanding is the frosting on the cake which can only be enjoyed by those sensitive enough to grasp it, and which challenges the consummate skills of the interpreter.

GEORGE B. HARTZOG, JR.
Director
National Park Service

Washington, D.C.
April, 1967

Preface to the Second Edition

IF I may be pardoned a personal reference, I wish to tell briefly what happened at a session of a national historical organization at which I happened to be presiding nearly three decades ago. In some way the group got around to discussing what might be done to make history more intelligible to the man on the street, and some of those present even dared to express the opinion that professional historians were not doing all they could and probably should do toward that end. After several minutes of this, a certain prominent historian of the old school, unable longer to bear listening to such heresy, ostentatiously pushed back his chair, got up, and stalked from the room, banging the door after him.

Such an attitude was typical of that of many professional historians and other scholars of the early twentieth century. Under the influence of the German graduate schools, such professionals had sought to become more and more scientific in their research and writing, with the result that their publications had tended to become more and more abstruse. Their works came to be filled with tremendous numbers of footnotes, and it had almost reached the point where the *summum bonum*, the ultimate, in scholarly achievement was to produce a page that contained only one line of text while all the remainder was filled with one or more erudite footnotes.

The scholar, indeed, seemed to care less and less whether the products of his researches were intelligible to anyone except a few other scholars. Woe to any so-called scholar who attempted to make his writings understandable to the general reader, and if you wanted to damn a scholar, all you had to do was to dub him a "popularizer." One distinguished historian is said to have remarked that if historical writing could be understood by the ordinary man it simply was not good history.

Likewise, until recent years most of our museums were stuffy and lacking in popular appeal, mere masses of ill-assorted oddities that had been brought in because someone happened to take a fancy to them. Even in some of our largest museums, with their great research collections, those in charge had learned little or nothing regarding attractive methods of display, extension programs, and the like. Not too long ago in one of our best-known museums an intramural argument was being conducted as to whether staff members should be pressured to engage extensively in research and to publish. One is reminded of the situation in many universities where the faculty member is almost obliged to "produce," to publish, if he is to receive recognition and promotion. In the case of a museum or park or historic site, however, administrative pressure on the individual staff member to "produce" seems to miss the point completely. A primary function and purpose of such an organization would seem to be to conduct a broad program for the public at large. Such a program will no doubt result in many "scholarly" publications. But for the administration to pressure individual staff members to "produce" such publications would seem to indicate that the administration itself needs to sweep the cobwebs out of its brain, to wake up and learn about recent far-reaching developments, about new methods and new techniques, in the broad field of museums, parks, and historic sites.

If for a long time the professional maintained an ivory-tower attitude, the amateur nevertheless continued to be interested and active in history and allied subjects. By the thousands amateurs delved into these subjects, and in the aggregate they published far more than did the professionals. The quality was not always of the best, but the interest and enthusiasm were most certainly there.

Thus there developed a vast chasm between the professional and the amateur—a gap, in fact, between the professional and the people at large. On the one hand the professional was up in the clouds and would not deign to come down and fraternize with ordinary mortals; he scorned and ridiculed the sometimes awkward and bungling attempts of the amateur. On the other hand the amateur kept trying, and millions of people kept on being interested. It was a bad situation, and something clearly needed to be done about it.

Fortunately, within recent years various individuals and groups on both sides of the chasm have seen the need and have sought to get together. Professional scholars in the fields of both history and the natural sciences have made an effort to present their works in a form more intelligible to laymen, and (perhaps partly as a result) the general public has become more interested in many of these fields. Likewise, amateurs have sought to be more careful in their writings, and often professionals have attempted to assist them, so that the quality of amateur products has undoubtedly improved. The public has been reached through books, newspapers, magazines, radio, television, and other means. One of the most striking examples of how one of the social studies can be made vividly interesting and can win large-scale popular approval and support is the book-magazine, *American Heritage*, that, even in a period when many of the older periodicals have been faltering or even succumbing, has been able to build up a large circulation. Related to this is the popular response to the Walt Disney films that deal with various phases of natural history.

It has come to be realized that in our modern complex world the formal education of youth in schools and colleges is not enough. Neither is the more or less formal education of adults, now so popular and so much talked about, sufficient to meet the great need. It is not enough to take a course in some subject. With the body of knowledge constantly broadening and deepening, we need to keep on learning, as youth and adults, formally and informally. There is so infinitely much that we would never learn from formal courses, and yet many of us have an insatiable appetite for knowledge. Various new mass media, such as those mentioned above, can help satisfy that appetite.

And now has come this new channel, this new means of reaching our people, through their parks, their museums, and their historic sites. In 1964, the visitor total for our national and state parks was more than 365,000,000. This development has made possible a new channel of mass communication, a new means of reaching our populace. It is a great and wonderful opportunity.

This new opportunity lies in the realm of what has come to be called "interpretation"—using the word with a special meaning. What that meaning is, we will not attempt to explain at this point, for a full and adequate explanation is given in the pages that follow. Suffice it to say that within recent years the workers at historic sites, in parks, and in museums have developed new and very effective techniques and methods of telling their story. In the spirit of trial and error they have experimented with first one device and then another. They have been traveling a road that has never been traveled before. In the beginning they were not certain just where they were going, and even today they are not entirely sure just where the final end will be. But wherever they may be going, they know—and we know—that it is toward a goal of marked significance, that they are on the highroad to real achievement.

In developing this new program, these workers have experimented with many things: with markers and inscriptions of various types, with different methods of restoring or reconstructing historic buildings, with ingenious maps and dioramas, with gadgets of different kinds. They have tried out devices that the visitor himself can operate and thereby come to feel that he is part of the picture that is being presented. They have introduced special lighting and sound effects. In toto they have tried out scores and hundreds of devices in order that objects might become to the visitor seeable and hearable, sometimes also feelable and smellable, and perhaps even tastable.

Did all these things just happen? Did they come into being without rhyme or reason? Obviously they did not. They are merely evidence of a new approach, a new philosophy. This latter is interpretation, the effort to make real and vivid to our people our common heritage in history and science and nature.

The present study does not include detailed instructions on how to restore a historic building or plan an exhibit or do many other things: such information can be obtained elsewhere. It does attempt to present an explanation of what is meant by the new interpretation and of what the workers in the field are trying to do. It seeks, that is, to interpret interpretation.

The study owes much to the experience and thinking of the professional staff of one of the agencies of our government, the National

Park Service of the Department of the Interior. Clearly it will be useful to the staff of that organization. It will have, however, a much wider appeal. To all, whether amateurs or professionals, who are interested or working in museums, in parks, in historic houses, and the like, it will be provocative and worthwhile. Undoubtedly it will be interesting and stimulating to many general readers.

To the author and to all who have assisted in the preparation of this work, we owe a debt of gratitude. Their study, insofar as we know, is the first that undertakes to cover this field. It is not the final word, as the author and his associates would be the first to admit. But it has gone far toward opening up new and fascinating horizons.

CHRISTOPHER CRITTENDEN
*North Carolina Department of
Archives and History*

Raleigh, N.C.
April, 1967

PART ONE

I have been careful to retain as much idiom as I could, often at the peril of being called ordinary and vulgar. Nations in a state of decay lose their idiom, which loss is always precursory to that of freedom. . . . Every good writer has much idiom; it is the life and spirit of language: and none such ever entertained a fear or apprehension that strength and sublimity were to be lowered and weakened by it. . . . Speaking to the people, I use the people's phraseology.

Demosthenes to Eubulides,
in *Imaginary Conversations*
of Walter Savage Landor

CHAPTER I

Principles of Interpretation

T HE WORD interpretation as used in this book refers to a public
service that has so recently come into our cultural world that
a resort to the dictionary for a competent definition is fruitless.
Besides a few obsolete meanings, the word has several special implications still in common use: the translation from one language into
another by a qualified linguist; the construction placed upon a legal
document; even the mystical explanation of dreams and omens.

Yet every year millions of Americans visit the national parks
and monuments, the state and municipal parks, battlefield areas,
historic houses publicly or privately owned, museums great and
small—the components of a vast preservation of shrines and treasures in which may be seen and enjoyed the story of our natural and
man-made heritage.

In most of such places the visitor is exposed, if he chooses, to a
kind of elective education that is superior in some respects to that
of the classroom, for here he meets the Thing Itself—whether it be
a wonder of Nature's work, or the act or work of Man. "To pay
a personal visit to a historic shrine is to receive a concept such as
no book can supply," someone has said; and surely to stand at the
rim of the Grand Canyon of the Colorado is to experience a spiritual elevation that could come from no human description of the
colossal chasm.

Thousands of naturalists, historians, archeologists and other
specialists are engaged in the work of revealing, to such visitors as
desire the service, something of the beauty and wonder, the inspiration and spiritual meaning that lie behind what the visitor can with

his senses perceive. This function of the custodians of our treasures is called Interpretation.

Because of the fear of misconception arising from conflicting definitions of the word, and also because some have thought it a pretentious way of describing what they believe to be a simple activity, there has been objection to the use of the word "interpretation" even among those engaged in this newer device of education. For myself I merely say that I do not share this objection. I have never been able to find a word more aptly descriptive of what we middlemen, either in the National Park Service or in any institution employing the means, are attempting to do.

But all during the practice of this educational activity, whether science or art or something of both, there has existed a strange situation. Interpretation has been performed—excellent, good, fair, and unsatisfactory—with only a vague reference to any philosophy upon which Interpretation could be based.

I have heard some superb interpretation not only in the National Park Service areas, but in far lesser places, and have found by interrogation that the interpreter was aware of no principles, but was merely following his inspiration. I actually believe that if there were enough pure inspiration in the world to go around, this might be the best way to perform the service. But we are not so cluttered with genius as all that. You have only to attend some of the worse performances in interpretation to wish heartily that there were some teachable principles, and perhaps some schools for interpreters.

This book results from a study of Interpretation as practiced in the many and diverse cultural preserves I have mentioned and from an inquiry as to whether there is such a philosophy, whether there are such basic principles, upon which the interpreter may proceed with an assurance that, though he may not be inspired, he will do an adequate job.

Since the earliest cultural activities of man there have been interpreters. Every great teacher has been an interpreter. The point is that he has seldom recognized himself specifically as such, and his interpretation has been personal and implicit as a part of his instruction. In a sermon called "A Christmas Message," Harry Emerson Fosdick showed what seems to me a profound knowledge of the highest meaning of this word, in speaking of Jesus. He said: "There are two kinds of greatness. One lies in the genius of the gigantic individual who...shapes the course of history. The other has its basis in the genius of the *revealer*—the man or woman who uncovers something universal in the world that has always been here and that men have not known. This person's greatness is not so much in himself as in what he unveils...to reveal the universal is the highest kind of greatness in any realm."

The reason why our college men, in past decades, have spoken with such reverence and affection of certain of their teachers—such men as Copeland and Charles Eliot Norton of Harvard and Bumpus of Brown, to name just three among many—was because such men by universality of mind instinctively went behind the body of information to project the soul of things. One of his pupils said of Dr. Bumpus: "He thoroughly enjoyed his stay upon this planet, which he found so full of a number of things...and he enjoyed pointing out these things in a new light.... He never forgot that the *feeling* of an exhibit and the need for it to tell a story were quite as important as its factual truthfulness."

To take a slice of a tree like the giant sequoia, and to associate its growth rings with a time chart of our human history, was an idea that occurred to some master interpreter.

Since Interpretation is a growth whose effectiveness depends upon a regular nourishment by well-directed and discriminating research, this introductory chapter seems as good a place as any to stress the importance of that resource. In an article printed in the magazine *Antiques*, Edward P. Alexander of Colonial Williamsburg, speaking of historic preserves, wrote: "Research is a continuing need and the life blood of good preservations. Both historical authenticity and proper interpretation demand facts. Research is the way to obtain these facts. There is no substitute for it, and no historic preservation should be attempted without research."

Colonial Williamsburg itself offers an ideal example of this truth. Here it was possible, through the generosity of Mr. Rockefeller, to employ the skill and taste of the most competent researchers in many fields to the end of bringing to life accurately and beautifully a segment of our early American history.

In the National Park Service is found an abundance of proof of the statement, and not merely in the department of history. Research is responsible for the satisfactory and stimulating experience of the visitor to Crater Lake, where the interpretation takes the visitor beyond the point of his aesthetic joy toward a realization of the natural forces that have joined to produce the beauty around him. This experience is made possible through continuing research here, because the explanation first accepted of the origin of the mighty caldera was not that which is now generally held. Nor was the research at Crater Lake alone that of the geologist. Many other specialists, including the archeologist, had their part in revealing the facts.

The vivifying programs at the Custis-Lee Mansion in Arlington, Virginia, emerge from the painstaking efforts of the historian who was not content with large generalizations, but sought in the records of the two families a multitude of homely details that bring the Custises and Lees into touch with our own daily experience.

At Fort Necessity, associated with the young George Washington, "something was wrong with the picture," as we say, yet cursory observation and guess had failed to arrive at the facts. Indeed a palisade reconstruction had been based upon false premises. A Park Service archeologist who refused to give up, even though many times baffled, was finally able to depict this tiny frontier post as it really was.

It had been commonly said for many years that the Nelson bighorn sheep had entirely disappeared from the confines of Death Valley National Monument. Indeed, so it was believed by practically all except the sheep themselves, whose rather important numbers now are made a matter of fact through the efforts of a naturalist, Ralph Wells, who has "lived" with flocks of the animals in the furnace-hot summer of the Valley.

Dinosaur National Monument comes to mind readily in this regard; so, naturally, does Jamestown, where digging in preparation for the Exposition of 1957 made it finally possible to people

The social insects are good interpretive subjects. The visible beehive at Rock Creek Nature Center, Washington, D.C., is attractive to young and old.

Nature's greatest laboratory is the sea. A ranger naturalist tells small visitors about the role of the starfish in the ecology of Acadia's coastal waters.

A group of enthusiastic youngsters scramble up a granite slope on a children's nature walk in Tuolumne Meadows, Yosemite National Park.

Ranger naturalist Carl Sharsmith shows how you can make a monkey flower move by tickling it with a pine needle.

Bright eyes find many interesting things in the meadow!

The river may carry this sand, worn from the granite rocks, all the way to the Pacific Ocean.

A lodgepole-pine forest is a good place to rest and listen to a nature story.

that little first settlement of the English-speaking colonists and give the ancient inhabitants flesh on their bones and blood in their veins.

When I consider what competent research can do in a yawning void, my mind goes to Fort Frederica, in Georgia, for it is natural for us to draw upon impressions that are gained at first hand. Previous to the work of the archeologist, teamed with the historian, at Oglethorpe's colony on the sea-island near Brunswick, I attempted some volunteer interpretation there at a time when there was not sufficient personnel present to aid the visitors. Charming as was that ancient ruin, with its live oaks and soothing estuary frontage, I found it almost impossible to make it real. I knew the historical background well enough, but the eyes of the visitors constantly wandered from me. I knew what they were thinking: "What was it like?" The structural relics were not imposing. The mounds might be those of earthwalls, but they did not register.

Well, I went to Frederica again, after the diggers had uncovered the site of the Hawkins-Davison houses, and again I had the pleasure of telling the story of Frederica to certain groups. What a difference those bricks and those exposed walls made! Somebody had lived here; this was part of a town; it now had a being.

Some years ago, in scrambling up a steep hillside of the Jemez Mountains of New Mexico, I found the ground well strewn with petrified marine shells of several species. I was at an elevation of not less than seven thousand feet. The discovery did not surprise me in the least; but it did made me wonder what the prehistoric Americans who must have seen such shells had thought about them. I knew that I was standing somewhere near the shoreline of a shallow sea that occupied this spot at a time before the land had been slowly upraised. How did I know this? The story had been interpreted for me; seemingly unrelated facts had been reasoned into a whole picture that solved all difficulties.

For dictionary purposes, to fill a hiatus that urgently needs to be remedied, I am prepared to define the function called Interpretation by the National Park Service, by state and municipal parks, by museums and similar cultural institutions as follows:

An educational activity which aims to reveal meanings and relationships through the use of original objects, by firsthand experience, and by illustrative media, rather than simply to communicate factual information.

This, let me emphasize, is for the dictionary, which logically attempts only an objective definition of words as they are, or have been, commonly accepted. The true interpreter will not rest at any dictionary definition. Besides being ready in his information and studious in his use of research, he goes beyond the apparent to the real, beyond a part to a whole, beyond a truth to a more important truth.

So, for the consideration of the interpreter, I offer two brief concepts of Interpretation, one for his private contemplation, and the other for his contact with the public. First, for himself: Interpretation is the revelation of a larger truth that lies behind any statement of fact.

The other is more correctly described as an admonition, perhaps: Interpretation should capitalize mere curiosity for the enrichment of the human mind and spirit.

In the matter of definition, I have tried to arrive at something upon which we can fairly well agree. We are seldom entirely happy with the utmost pains of the lexicographer: we find words given as synonymous that we do not so consider; a definition is too inclusive, or it fails to emphasize that which we believe is vital. As to the concepts given above, I should hope that the interpreter will have others of his own, doubtless just as valid and just as stimulating. If we can agree upon principles, the stress and shading of the individual will be no impairment but a reflection of his true appreciation of those principles.

Now, what are these principles? I find six bases that seem enough to support our structure. There is no magic in the number six. It may be that my reader will point out that some of these principles interfinger. It may be that he will feel that, after all, there is but one, and all the others are corollary. On the other hand, since I am ploughing a virgin field so far as a published philosophy of the subject is concerned, some of my readers may be provoked into adding further furrows. Very well. This book pretends to no finality, no limitation. We are clearly engaged in a new kind of group education based upon a systematic kind of preservation and use of national cultural resources. The scope of this activity has no counterpart in older nations or other times.

I believe that interpretive effort, whether written or oral or projected by means of mechanical devices, if based upon these six principles, will be correctly directed. There will inevitably be differences in excellence arising from varied techniques and from the personality of the interpreter. Obviously I cannot be concerned with those factors in such a book as this. The National Park Service has an extensive Manual and a number of admirable booklets for the governance of the spot-conduct of both the interpreter and his interpretation.

Here, then, are the six principles:

I. Any interpretation that does not somehow relate what is being displayed or described to something within the personality or experience of the visitor will be sterile.

II. Information, as such, is not Interpretation. Interpretation is revelation based upon information. But they are entirely different things. However, all interpretation includes information.

III. Interpretation is an art, which combines many arts, whether the materials presented are scientific, historical or architectural. Any art is in some degree teachable.

IV. The chief aim of Interpretation is not instruction, but provocation.

V. Interpretation should aim to present a whole rather than a part, and must address itself to the whole man rather than any phase.

VI. Interpretation addressed to children (say, up to the age of twelve) should not be a dilution of the presentation to adults, but should follow a fundamentally different approach. To be at its best it will require a separate program.

I plan to make no generalizations in this book without the support of one or more illustrations or examples. My aim is clarity and succinctness, rather than style, even though I recommend that the interpreter never forget that "style" is a priceless ingredient of interpretation. "What is style?" somebody asked of a French writer.

"Le style, c'est l'homme," was the reply. (Style is just the man himself.) So style is just the interpreter himself. How does he give it forth? It emerges from love. We shall later have a little chapter upon love. I do not name it here as a principle. It is, indeed, not a principle but a passion.

CHAPTER II

The Visitor's First Interest

Any interpretation that does not somehow relate what is being displayed or described to something within the personality or experience of the visitor will be sterile.

> As we read, we must become Greeks, Romans, Turks, priest, king, martyr and executioner; must fasten these images to some reality in our secret experiences.—Ralph Waldo Emerson.

A ROSTER of the reasons why people visit parks, museums, historic houses and similar preserves, though a fascinating excursion into human psychology, need not detain us here. All interpreters know from their experiences that the reasons are so many and diverse that merely to name them all would take pages of this book.

I go upon the assumption therefore that whatever their reasons for coming, the visitors are there. What we should determine, then, if we aim at establishing our first principle of Interpretation is: Now that the visitor is here, in what will be his chief interest, and inevitably his chief interest, while he is with us?

The answer is: The visitor's chief interest is in whatever touches his personality, his experience and his ideals.

The adult visitor who happens to be the auditor or reader of interpretation has no general awe of the interpreter. He takes it for granted that the latter possesses special knowledge that he himself lacks, and he respects both that knowledge and the possessor of it (especially if he is in uniform) to exactly that extent. But he is not without his pride, or vanity if you wish, and he probably considers himself just as good an "all-around man" as his interlocutor. He does not so much wish to be talked *at* as to be talked *with*. He knows, and the interpreter knows, that this is not directly possible. It cannot be a round-table conversation. Hence we have to try to achieve something of this purpose in some oblique way. In a moment we shall see that there is definitely such an indirect means.

But first, as to the intimation that the visitor's chief interest is in something that concerns himself. This attitude of the adult is not to be confused with what we commonly know as selfishness. It not only is not the same thing—it need not even have much in common with it.

C. E. Merriam in his book "The Making of Citizens" has indicated the strength of the urge of men to associate themselves with the historic past:

The underlying design is of course to set up a group of the living, the dead, and those who are yet unborn, a group of which the individual finds himself a part and of which he is in fact glad to count himself a member, and by virtue of that fact an individual of no mean importance in the world. All the great group victories he shares in; all the great men are his companions in the bonds of the group; all its sorrows are by construction his; all its hopes and dreams, realized and thwarted alike, are his. And thus he becomes although of humble status a great man, a member of a great group; and his humble life is thus tinged with a glory it might not otherwise ever hope to achieve. He is lifted beyond and above himself into higher worlds where he walks with all his great ancestors, one of an illustrious group whose blood is in his veins and whose domain and reputation he proudly bears.

I once referred to interpreters, speaking of those in the National Park Service, as "middlemen of happiness." Of course, it is impossible for anyone to make someone else happy. "Le bonheur n'est pas une chose aisée," said Nicholas Chamfort. "Il est très difficile de le trouver dans nous, et impossible de le trouver ailleurs." (Happiness is not easy to come by. It is hard to find it within ourselves, and impossible to find it anywhere else.) Neither the sublime qualities of the primitive national parks, nor anything the interpreter can say about them, can make anyone happy; but the one and the other, happily teamed, can offer those elements by which people can bring to life their hidden capacities for happiness.

Generally speaking, certainties contribute toward human happiness; uncertainties are a source of spiritual loneliness and disquietude. Whether or not he is conscious of it, Man seeks to find his place in nature and among men—not excluding remote men. Primitive parks, the unspoiled seashore, archeological ruins, battlefields, zoological and botanical gardens, historic preservations—all happen to be exactly those places where this ambition is most likely to be satisfied. So, even though your visitor may not himself know just what immediate impulse brought him to any one of these places, he is for this ultimate reason in a receptive mood. To capitalize this mood, even if it arises from mere curiosity or whim, is a challenge to the interpreter.

The visitor is unlikely to respond unless what you have to tell, or to show, touches his personal experience, thoughts, hopes, way of life, social position, or whatever else. If you cannot connect his ego (I use the word in an inoffensive sense) with the chain of your revelation, he may not quit you physically, but you have lost his interest. Dr. John Merriam spoke of "that touch of presentation ... which relates it to personal interest." When a person reads a novel or sees a play, he instinctively measures the fictional behavior against what he imagines his own character and conduct, under such circumstances, would be.

In the museum, the interpreter can seldom come into contact with his visitor. In lieu of that, he must leave a message for him. Usually this will take the form of a label. Most interpreters have heard the statement of Dr. Brown Goode that "a museum is a well-arranged collection of labels, illustrated by specimens." I assume this to be a deliberate exaggeration to emphasize a truth. But the label certainly can be galvanic, or it can be inert. The label can project itself directly into the personality of the visitor to the exhibit, and make him feel a direct connection with what he sees. Two good examples of this I found in the Witte Museum in San Antonio, Texas. One label was on a large case that contained the skeleton of a mammoth: "Prehistoric mammoths were here in Texas just a few thousand years ago. They roamed the plains in great herds. . . . The chances are that they browsed right where you are standing now."

Where *you* are standing *now*. With that statement the mammoths are not far away creatures of time or space but right under your feet. Another gem from the same museum—this time on a case showing West Texas plants which were used by aboriginal Indians: "Do you need a water bucket? a pair of shoes? a blanket, floor mat or rope? If so, the materials in this case [sotol, lechuguilla, beargrass, devil's shoestring, etc.] will serve your purpose."

As he reads this label, and views these plants, the visitor is no longer wholly a foreigner to the prehistoric man. *He* would have had these needs. He would have supplied these needs with exactly these materials. He and They are brothers-under-the-skin. Certainly it would not be well to overwork this word "you." It would become offensive. There are plenty of ways to effect the same end. If labels can merge a plant exhibit with the personality of the visitor, surely the interpreter can do far more to that end when he has the privilege of direct contact.

A felicitous example of the knack of associating the object with some homely but keen sense of drama that lies within the visitor's personal range is to be found at the Franklin Delano Roosevelt homesite in Hyde Park, New York. It is in the room where the President was born. You could put up a label and say, "President Roosevelt was born in this room." That is accurate information. Or in personal contact with his group the interpreter would be at liberty to state the fact in any elaborated way he might please. But someone had an inspiration here. What you see is a reproduction of the telegram sent by the happy father, James Roosevelt, to a friend announcing the arrival in Hyde Park "of a bouncing boy, weight 9½ pounds, this morning." It is just what you or I would have done, and you instantly feel kinship not merely with the Roosevelts, but with the whole mansion and area.

For remember, the visitor ultimately is seeing things through his own eyes, not those of the interpreter, and he is forever and finally translating your words *as best he can* into whatever he can refer to his own intimate knowledge and experience. I put the words *as best he can* in italics, because thus it will emphasize the importance of making this translation as easy as possible. Words like dendrochronology and photosynthesis and biota, and excur-

One of a number of new visitor-information centers in the National Forests. Sawtooth National Forest, Idaho.

Interpretation in the National Forests focuses on the multiple-use concept.

Through an audio device visitors to Superior National Forest hear a French-Canadian "voyageur" tell of his arduous life in the fur trade of a bygone century.

A Forest Service visitor-information specialist uses a wedge and cones from the Sugar Pine to explain timber management in California.

Informal guided walks help visitors develop new understandings of the forest environment in Eldorado National Forest, California.

Reconstruction of Revolutionary War soldiers' huts aids interpretation at Valley Forge State Park, scene of several Boy Scout Jamborees.

sions into Latin taxonomy, not merely do not aid him, they throttle him. If, indeed, there were time to reveal the picture-quality of some of these apt technical words, they might appeal to the few, but I fear that the interpreter faces enough difficulties without further adding to them.

In most of what the interpreter may tell a visitor of prehistoric or modern man's activities, at peace or at war, the opportunity always arises to provoke in the mind of the hearer the questions, "What would *I* have done under similar circumstances? What would have been *my* fate?" Is the visitor at Lee Mansion, across the Potomac from Washington? Robert E. Lee never occupied this house for long. But in it was the scene of the great tragic moment when a man who loved the Union, and the United States army he had served, had to make a decision. Virginia was his mother. What should he do? What, given all those circumstances, would the visitor have done?

It may not be too much to say that most history may be interpreted effectively (but of course not exclusively) by provoking the thought, "Under like conditions what would *you* have done?"

Perhaps the visitor is being told of the atlatl, the throwing stick of the Southwest prehistoric Indian. Would the visitor have found out and applied a principle of physics that enabled him to "lengthen his arm," so to speak? Well, many of those visitors as children sharpened the end of a stick, thrust it into a green apple, and then hurled the apple much farther than they could have thrown it with the unaided arm and hand. That was a throwing stick, was it not?

Dr. Clark Wissler once said, "As a rule the visitor entering Mesa Verde the first time has no conception of prehistoric life in the Southwest. Everything looks strange and unexpected." Now, imagine the visitor to have come to a prehistoric Indian ruin on Thanksgiving Day, after a typical modern dinner. He would probably have been eating turkey, squash or pumpkin pie, and possibly corn bread or corn in some other form. At least sixteen articles of food in our present-day menu have come down to us from these aboriginal peoples, according to Dr. John Corbett. Here, for the visitor, is at once offered a vivid link with the past. Skilful interpretation goes on from there into homely parallels with our own day-to-day existence. These people of other centuries played, loved, quarreled, worshipped, knew beauty—all the essentials were about the same. The strangeness and unexpectedness mentioned by Dr. Wissler disappears. The visitor says, "These folks were not so different, after all."

Finally, so far as this chapter is concerned, I hope to clinch the nail with what I regard as a triumph of interpretation by Thomas Henry Huxley, one of the greatest of biologists.

Huxley engaged to deliver a series of lectures to Workingmen's Institutes in certain English cities. One of these talks was delivered in Norwich. Huxley called it "On a Piece of Chalk." It was such a superb bit of composition that it became a classic of English style, and appears in many anthologies. We are now not concerned with the style, but only with its superiority as Interpretation. Here are Huxley's opening words: "If a well were sunk at our feet in the midst of the city of Norwich, the diggers would very soon find themselves at work in that white substance almost too soft to be called rock, with which we are all familiar as 'chalk.'"

Consider this beginning—very free and easy, conversational, without a single suggestion that the speaker is one of the world's great men of science. The audience is immediately made a part of everything that is to follow. The well may be sunk right under where they are sitting. It will be *their* well, not a well in East Prussia. It is therefore *their* chalk. Only later will they learn that this bed of chalk extends three thousand miles to central Asia.

"A great chapter of the history of the world is written in the chalk." A little tug on the imagination, but not too much. Huxley brings it back home again: "Every Norwich carpenter carries a bit of this chalk in his pocket."

"The language of the chalk is not hard to understand. Not nearly as hard as Latin, if you only want to get at the broad features it has to tell...." Notice that phrase "it has to tell." Not "I want to tell you something you ought to know," but "the chalk will tell you something."

Now comes the masterpiece: "I propose that we now set to work to spell that story out together." From that moment, everything Huxley is going to tell his audience (and most of it was entirely novel to them) is going to be like a discovery they are about to make, with Huxley going along as a sort of companion.

"The world exists," said Emerson, "for the education of each man. There is no age, or state of society, or mode of action in history, to which there is not something corresponding in his own life."

CHAPTER III

Raw Material and Its Product

*Information, as such, is not Interpretation. Interpretation
is revelation based upon information. But they are entirely
different things. However, all interpretation includes
information.*

> The simple fact that a great battle was won or
> lost makes little impression on our mind...
> while our imagination and attention are alike
> excited by the detailed description of a much
> more trifling event.... This must ever be the
> case while we prefer a knowledge of man-
> kind to a mere acquaintance with their actions.
> —Sir Walter Scott, in introduction to *Froissart.*

THE NATIONAL PARK SERVICE has, for the guidance of its personnel, an exhaustive Administrative Manual. A section of this
Manual deals with "Information and Interpretation in the Field."
Speaking of "Newspaper Publicity" at the area level, one of the
injunctions to the employee is as follows: "Do not editorialize in
a news story. Stick to statements of fact, which can include the
fact that somebody, identified in the story, expressed an opinion
which is germane to the story."

Of course this would be accepted by anyone as prudent advice.
It means, in effect, do not try to interpret: merely inform.

Let me try to give an illustration of how this policy works out
in the case of the newspaper itself. When Adolph Ochs was the
owner and manager of the *New York Times*, he took what may be
termed a purist attitude as to the place of information and interpretation in his newspaper. To him, it was not proper that his reporters

should go beyond writing the facts, so far as it is humanly possible to ascertain the facts. Interpretation of the news belonged to the editorial page. It is inescapable that a reporter, who after all is a human being, could not altogether avoid imprinting his personality upon even a cold recital. But this was the ideal of the *Times* under Ochs.

Exactly the opposite view, in the newspaper world, was that of Dana and Laffan of the *New York Sun*. The reporter was not merely given leave, he was encouraged, in the interest of readability, to "make a good story" of an event. As a result the *Sun*, which was often called a newspaperman's newspaper, always sparkled, while the writing fraternity, even though they respected the Ochs ideal, called the *Times* colorless.

The San Francisco earthquake of 1906 supplied a fine test of the two journalistic points of view. For many hours the stricken city was cut off from the world. In such a case, dependence is always upon rumor, opinion, and stray leakage of "facts" (usually not facts at all). The *Times* strove diligently in its news columns to maintain its ideal. But the *Sun* had on its staff a brilliant newspaperman named Will Irwin, who was a San Franciscan. The "news" story written by Irwin will always be a classic of journalism. The earthquake facts did not bother Will. All he knew was that his beloved city at the Golden Gate was broken and burning. He and his brother Wallace (also a writer) had been happy there in the fleecy fog that rolled in, of afternoons, down to Van Ness Avenue; they had feasted joyously at the Poodle Dog in its palmy days; they had jinked with the Bohemians. Will poured out his heart in a "story" that interpreted the very essence of his city. People that had never been there felt that they, too, had leaned against a lamppost on Market Street, and had idled in the picturesque Chinese quarter around Grant Avenue. They saw, felt, and heard—and lamented the loss of something that had instantly become theirs. This was Interpretation: the revelation of the soul of a city. It was based upon fact, but they were not the facts of the earthquake destruction. I imagine Mr. Ochs of the *Times* enjoyed this Irwin tour de force as much as anyone, but he might not have printed it.

He believed that information was one thing, and interpretation was another, and seldom the twain should meet.

It is an idle quibble to point out that the interpreter may, and indeed in most cases must, dispense pure information; or that, conversely, the man who gives information may indulge in words that are actually interpretive. The same dual role can exist in the roadside sign or the label, and normally should be present in printed matter. It is only necessary to keep in mind that they are dual roles; that information and interpretation are essentially two different things.

When Charles Darwin was a young man, he made a voyage of nearly five years in a British warship. The account of that circumnavigation of the globe was published under the title of *The Cruise of the Beagle*, and has become so much a classic for the lay reader that it is included in Everyman's Library. Many a person who has never gone through *The Origin of Species* or the *Earthworm* has taken delight in the *Beagle*.

In this book, Darwin shows that the man of science can be also a great interpreter, with a subtle sense of what is needed to make scientific discovery and research come alive to the average man. His picture of the degraded natives of Tierra del Fuego has almost fictional allure.

In South America Darwin was at one time in the Uspallata Range of the Cordilleras. He described the topography and the geology of this area—straight information. "It consists," he wrote, "of various kinds of submarine lava, alternating with volcanic sandstones and other sedimentary deposits...from this resemblance to the tertiary beds on the shores of the Pacific I expected to find silicified wood." He did find such wood; they were firs, of the Araucarian family, with some affinity to the yew.

Thus far, this was information, and specialized. You could not expect the layman to become very enthusiastic about the statement. But Darwin proceeds:

It required very little geological practice to interpret the marvellous story which this scene at once unfolded....I saw the spot where a cluster of fine trees once waved their branches on the shores of the Atlantic, when that ocean came to the foot of the Andes.

I saw that they had sprung from a volcanic soil which had been raised from the level of the sea, and that subsequently this dry land, with its upright trees, had been let down into the depths of the ocean. In these depths the formerly dry land was covered by sedimentary beds and these again by enormous streams of submarine lava. . . .

But again the subterranean forces exerted themselves, and I now beheld the bed of that ocean forming a chain of mountains more than 7000 feet in height . . . nor had the antagonist forces been dormant, which are always at work wearing down the surface of the land: the great piles of strata had been intersected by many wide valleys, and the trees, now changed into silex, were exposed projecting from the volcanic soil, now changed into rock, whence formerly, in green and budding state, they had raised their lofty heads. Now, all is utterly irreclaimable and desert; even the lichen cannot adhere to the stony casts of former trees.

If anyone points out that in this graphic interpretation of the facts Darwin was still employing certain words that would be unfamiliar to many readers, that is true. But it must be remembered that the words were meant to be read, not spoken, and book reading implies the opportunity to look up words in the dictionary, when the interest is excited. At any rate, it seems to me a grand example of Interpretation, manifesting the difference between what is informative and what is interpretive. When Darwin used the word "interpret" he showed plainly that he, at least, never confused the two things.

Robert F. Griggs, of Ohio State University, the leader of the Mount Katmai expeditions of 1915 and 1916, gave in his fascinating article written for the *National Geographic Magazine* a perfect example of that felicitous touch of interpretation which relates the unfamiliar to the familiar in the mind of reader or auditor.

Katmai had erupted in June, 1912. It was one of the most tremendous volcanic explosions of all time, as may be judged by the estimated five cubic miles of ash and pumice belched into the air. But Katmai was far away, even the name being unfamiliar to most people. To say what the effect of this eruption was upon the country around it would be likewise speaking of a vague territory sparsely inhabited. But Griggs found a way to make it real.

Imagine, advised the writer, a "similar outburst" centered in New York City. "In such a catastrophe all of Greater New York would be buried under ten to fifteen feet of ash and subjected to the unknown horrors from hot gases. The column of steam would be plainly visible beyond Albany.... Philadelphia would be covered by a foot of gray ash and would grope in total darkness for sixty hours. Washington and Baltimore would receive a quarter of an inch.... The sounds of the explosion would be heard as far as Atlanta and St. Louis. The fumes would be noticed as far as Denver, San Antonio and Jamaica."

This device of interpretation, brought home, could be used in giving an adequate notion of the magnitude of our great Columbia Basin lava flow. Pick up that lava, so to speak, and lay it down east of the Mississippi, where the concentration of population and development is greatest. "Here is what, if it happened now, it would bury and destroy...."

In his book called "Life on the Mississippi," Mark Twain, in the very first chapter, showed that he knew what Interpretation is. After stating that De Soto saw the river in the year 1542, Twain wrote:

To say that De Soto saw it in 1542 is a remark which states a fact without interpreting it: it is something like giving the dimensions of a sunset by astronomical measurements and cataloguing the colors by their scientific names—as a result you get the bald fact of the sunset, but you don't see the sunset.

The date standing by itself means little or nothing to us; but when one groups a few neighboring historical dates and facts around it, he adds perspective and color.... for instance, when the Mississippi was first seen by a white man, less than a quarter of a century had elapsed since Francis I's defeat at Pavia; the death of Raphael, the death of Bayard ... Catherine de Medici was a child; Elizabeth of England was not yet in her teens ... Shakespeare was not yet born....

There is not room here to reproduce the whole long paragraph. It is enough to say that (as was Twain's intent) after you read the list of associated events, you have perspective: the year 1542 has ceased to be merely a calendar entry.

Certainly the raw material of interpretation is information. My

National Park Service, Richard Frear

By providing opportunities for personal interaction with the resources,
the park interpreter encourages visitors to interpret for themselves.
Acadia National Park, Maine.

Interpretation at Cape Hatteras National Seashore, North Carolina, is enhanced by the drama of sailing days, when this barrier beach was known as "the graveyard of the Atlantic."

Visitors ride a mule-drawn barge on the historic Chesapeake and Ohio Canal through Georgetown while a park historian tells the story of this important nineteenth-century trade route.

The Liberty Bell has meaning for all. Interpreting it can bring several senses into use—sight, hearing, and touch. Independence National Historical Park.

In the National Park Service Museum Laboratory, skilled craftsmen and artists create dioramas that give a surprising suggestion of reality.

A finished diorama depicts Elkhorn Ranch, Theodore Roosevelt National Memorial Park, North Dakota.

quotations from Huxley, Twain and Griggs have shown that the researcher himself may be a fine interpreter. But this is only to say that some men can play dual roles superbly. It is not a just expectation of the scientific worker that he should be expert in both the science and the art. The interpreter begins where the decision has finally been made: "This is what we think proper to call the facts."

There are cases where, after long study, the specialists are not agreed as to what are the facts. "What," asked Dr. Schroeder of me one day, "are you going to do, as to your public interpretation, where two competent archeologists draw opposite conclusions from a body of evidence?" My answer is that the man engaged in interpretation (the kind with which this book deals) must wait for authoritative decision from some source. Sometimes, where good authorities differ, he may well present both sides. When the matter is of such tremendous import that he must tell a story about it, as in the case of the Pleistocene glaciation, he may frankly say that nobody knows the precise answer; such an occasional statement sometimes produces a feeling of added confidence in the hearer.

In Acadia National Park, aside from the scenic land-and-sea beauty, the visitor is primarily interested in the many physical evidences that the land was once deeply covered by a slowly moving sheet of ice. There are many hypotheses as to what caused this glaciation in North America and Europe; none is, of itself alone, satisfactory. In such a case, true interpretation need not be hampered. Indeed, the visitor, after being frankly informed that nobody knows the ultimate cause, may be induced (we are all challenged by puzzles) to do some thinking about it himself; even if his thinking is unscientific, his horizon cannot fail to be widened. In a region of the blind a one-eyed man may become king.

The work of the specialist, the historian, the naturalist, the archeologist, is fundamental, then. Without their research the interpreter cannot start. But you sometimes note an impatience on the part of a specialist that the public does not show sufficient interest in his assemblage of information as such. He is likely to conclude that the average person is somewhat stupid. The opposite is true. It is a sign of native intelligence on the part of any person not to clutter his mind with indigestibles. "We find it to be a law," said James John Garth Wilkinson, a great English surgeon, "when a branch of knowledge has been cultivated for ages and still remains inaccessible to the world at large, that its principles are not high or broad enough, and that something radically deeper is demanded. If it does not interest universal man, that is sufficient to prove the point."

The "something radically deeper" is an art form—an analogy, a parable, a picture, a metaphor—something that "brings things down and incarnates them," as Wilkinson said. This art form, for our purpose, takes the shape of Interpretation.

Comprised within the National Park System, as well as within state and other preservations, are many places that must carry to the visitor some broad impression of the toil, the sacrifice, the intelligence and the conflict that is part of our national history. Let us take, for example, the cluster of Civil War battlefields and related areas. In the fifty years following the end of that fratricidal war, there was much emphasis, when the veterans and their children were visiting the scenes of each bloody combat, upon information. It was then a thrill to know, to recall, just where papa's regiment had stood, by what road an advance or retreat was made. It is true, of course, that under the circumstances then existing, the mere recital of information could have been in some degree an interpretation.

Now that we approach the centenary of the outbreak of the war, it becomes increasingly clear that the visitor's interest is not so much in the military details, but in the great human story: "Why did men act as they did? How would I act under such circumstances? What does it all mean to me?"

It is true that there are exceptions to this general statement. The historian in one of these areas must be prepared to deal with the informative as well as the interpretive. A group of Civil War Round Table enthusiasts will be interested in specific details of a battle; so will students preparing a paper; so may younger school groups where the visit is intended to reveal, perhaps, the part played by the troops of a state or locality. But these are the exceptions, and insofar as they are, they are not Interpretation. Jacques Barzun, the historian, has stated the case boldly and well:

However stupid or uneducated, the most indifferent citizen will remember and respond to certain ideas connected with his country's past. Lincoln's log cabin may suggest the heroism of western pioneers or it may mean that humble birth is no bar to high office.... To a Frenchman you need not explain Joan of Arc. The intricate details of her career, trial and death, are as nothing compared with the image that spells patriotism, kingship and sainthood.

"The historian," continues Barzun, "who forgets his duty is the one who attempts the treatment of an actual historical question and thinks he has achieved it when he has only rummaged into the past and exhibited his finds.... The use of History is not external but internal. Not what you can do with history, but what history does to you, is its use."

Finally, I wish to quote something from Liddell Hart, in a preface to his book on General W. T. Sherman:

Those accustomed to the conventional history and biography may complain that the account of battles is uncomfortably bare and scantily furnished with details....

To place the position and trace the action of battalions and batteries is only of value to the collector of antiques, and still more to the dealer in faked antiques.... This book is a study of life, not of still life. An exercise in human pyschology, not in upholstery.

I do not subscribe to the tone of asperity employed; but I think the comment not only has merit, but sharply points out that true Interpretation deals not with parts, but with a historical—and I would say spiritual—whole.

CHAPTER IV

The Story's the Thing

*Interpretation is an art, which combines many arts,
whether the materials presented are scientific, historical
or architectural. Any art is in some degree teachable.*

> The professor threw himself down upon the
> sofa and moaned: "I am a hopeless failure as a
> teacher."
> "This is just the dejection of a moment, my
> dearest," said his wife, gently. "Why should
> you think yourself a failure?"
> "It is not momentary. I have seen it for some
> time. For months my pupils have shown an
> interest in everything I tell them."
> A great joy shone in the woman's eyes. "I have
> known it always," she cried. "You are a poet! I
> am so happy you have found it out at last.
> We shall now starve happily together."—Pedro
> Sarráchaca, *El Pedagogo Vascongado.*

SOON OR LATE the interpreter must face the question of whether
he is dealing with a science or an art. Interpretation is one or
the other; it cannot be both. If it is an art, it can draw upon all
science. But if it is a science, it can have no patience with "the sweet
insouciance of lettered ease." Dr. John Merriam remarked of Albert
Michelson, the physicist, that "it was his lot to be a scientist, otherwise he would have been a great artist." The very fact that Michelson chose to be the one rather than the other is sufficient to indicate
that in practice they are not compatible.

Someone—perhaps Whitehead—referred to education as "knowledge treated imaginatively." Science cannot afford to treat knowl-

edge imaginatively in the sense that the artist can, though great scientists are men of high imagination. So, if you regard education as a science, the only way the educator can achieve such an end is to turn to art. The teacher of arithmetic must insist that two and two make four. H. G. Wells proposed that there is actually no such thing in life as "two." Therefore, he said, the truth is that "a little more or less than two plus a little more or less than two, equals a little more or less than four." Wells was speaking as an artist. He was treating knowledge imaginatively. The public accountant will go right on insisting that bookkeepers had better avoid art, except as an avocation.

"Use materials as the basis for education," said Merriam, "but treat them imaginatively." You cannot treat the materials imaginatively without giving them form. This is what Heinrich Heine had in mind when he lamented, concerning his fellow Germans: "Thanks to the conscientious exactitude with which we are bent, we compilers never think about the form that will best represent any particular fact."

Dr. Merriam implied, when he used the word "education," a much higher service than the teaching of facts. He yearned, in our national parks, for an appeal to the emotions, to the hunger for deeper understanding, to the religious spirit of the individual, no less than to the love of beautiful and wonderful objects, or the restoration of physical well being.

I can't attempt to tell you what I think about Nature. Probably your reactions are like mine. But the point is ... that the contribution of science gives a vision of the continuity of law which looks like a purpose in Nature, that makes our relation to Nature—all the way from contact with the clod to the tree or to the mountain—in one sense that of companionship. I am inclined to think that the poets have come closer to the appreciation of what this means than any other group of people.

It will be obvious at this point where we are driving. We have already given up the notion that Interpretation, in the sense we are employing the word, is direct education. Now, then, we may as well plump it right out: The interpreter must use art, and at best he will be somewhat of a poet. This sounds frightening, I allow. I can see some of my readers shuddering at the thought and wondering where it leaves them. "But I never wrote a line of poetry in my life. You cannot expect me to be an artist."

I reply: You do not know yourself. You have been so frustrated by the curatorship of unimportant details that you have forgotten your inborn talent. We are all, in some degree, poets and artists. If you mean you are not capable of the exquisite flights of a John Keats or the rumbling organ tones of a Thomas Hardy, very well. None of us are. But we can have something of the perception of a poet without having the graphic skill. We can have a sense of joy at sounding a lovely chord, without being a virtuoso.

I once made a long automobile trip with a businessman. We had been on the road only a few hours when I came to the sour conclusion that the adventure was a mistake for both of us. Either he was prosaically dull or I was intellectually a bore, or both. I could elicit nothing but sodden commonplaces from him. It was developing into a mobile nightmare. But we finally came to western New England—the Berkshire Hills—and it was springtime. My companion had never been that far East before. He suddenly stopped the car on a hillside and sat for a moment looking at the white birches, with greening leaves. Then he said, "Look! Those trees seem to be all racing down the hill to wash their feet in the creek." And, reacting to his poetic impression, I began to see exactly what he saw. Out of this humdrum John had popped something as lovely as an old Greek myth.

If a nymph had appeared it would not have surprised me.

You just never can tell how much artistic perception people may have in their depths. The interpreter who uses art, creating a "story" out of his materials, will find himself in the presence of people who have the artistic appreciation to understand him.

I am sure that what I am saying will not be misconstrued to mean that the interpreter should be any sort of practicing artist: that he should read poems, give a dramatic performance, deliver an oration, become a tragic or comic thespian, or anything as horribly out of place as these. Nothing could be worse, except perhaps to indulge in an evangelical homily. I am merely suggesting that he dip into his own artistic appreciation, give form and life to his material, and tell a story rather than recite an inventory. The whole history of entertainment reminds us that a dull performance has a dull audience; and while we must be chary of that word "entertainment," and be sure we restrict ours to the very highest kind, we cannot forget that people are with us mainly seeking enjoyment, not instruction.

The makers of the ancient myths, as G. K. Chesterton reminds us, cultivated the "images that were adventures of the imagination," and "they best understood that the soul of a landscape is a story, and the soul of a story is a personality."

What makes me sure that I am right about this is the fact, so well known to me, that there are many interpreters in the National Park Service who have come to such a conclusion, perhaps before I myself did. Harry C. Parker wrote me some years ago (in guarded terms, fearing I might misunderstand him), "I sometimes believe that interpretation...is more of an art than a science." Merrill Mattes ventures a modest belief that "to do a really good job, a writer must have an instinct for compression of words found mainly among poets and advertising men." The "instinct for compression" is, after all, just another way of describing form. The artist ruthlessly cuts away all the material that is not vital to his story.

I have heard so many wise statements concerning the necessity for "telling a story" from interpreters now within the National Park Service that for a long time I have wondered why they did not put their own convictions into their practice. I can only suppose that they have been reluctant to be thought innovators. But if, indeed, they have not been quite convinced that they were right, I hope that my affirmation will give them as much courage as theirs has given me.

It is probably true that the professional writer will always be able to score more hits in the production of interpretive literature, of markers and labels, than the nonprofessional. At the same time the professional can sometimes be so hypnotized by his own skill and by his affection for phrasing that he touches only the brain and does not reach the heart. For that reason, I wholly agree with James W. Holland when he says that excellent texts might sometimes be written by "a superintendent or a clerk, an engineer or a ranger, or even a member of the maintenance force." Therefore, I likewise partly agree with J. C. Harrington that "many now in the Service could do an adequate job—if they could and would take the time." I regard Interpretation as a teachable art; therefore I do not think it is at all a matter of "taking time." All the time in the world is insufficient unless the principles are understood. All the good intentions are unavailing unless the interpreter understands that form is the essence, and that pedagogical miscellany is a bore to the man on holiday.

To the specialist the use of metaphor is calamitous, and simile is almost an obscenity. Analogy may be employed, but only for the purpose of further perplexing a student. I am not saying that, within his limited educational orbit, the specialist is not right about this. I rather assume he is. But he must realize that this abhorrence of artistic form is exactly why, in speaking to a lay audience, he can empty a room more quickly than a cry of "Fire!"

The lifeblood of satisfying interpretation flows from the proper and ingenious use of exactly those devices of language that take the hearer or reader beyond the observed fact to, or at least toward, a certification of spirit. "I disbelieve," said Garth Wilkinson, in ringing tones that are fit to be engraved on the memory of every interpreter, "in what is called the severity, strictness and dryness of science...we have found practically that metaphor is a sword of the spirit, and whenever a great truth is fixed, it is by some happy metaphor that it is willing to inhabit for a time: and again, that whenever a long controversy is ended, it is by one of the parties getting hand on a metaphor whose blade burns with the runes of Truth."

The King James version of the Bible, which has been the model of many a master of simple and effective composition, is a storehouse of these "burning blades." Lincoln's Gettysburg Address flows straight from his youthful devotion to this marvel of English style. Suppose Mr. Lincoln had devoted an hour at Gettysburg to a closely reasoned and brilliant analysis of the relative strategy of Meade and Lee. Do you think his talk would now have been graven on bronze?

You may have had the experience of going out for an evening

and having your host, or perhaps your hostess, begin to regale the party with "a story you will be interested in." Something that really happened to us last August—or was it September? We were on our way to—where was it, Emily? No it couldn't have been that place; that was another time. The story drags along, with interruptions caused by recalling this queer thing about Uncle Henry, and that perfectly gorgeous view from a mountain top in where-was-it—no, that was the year before. The narrative begins to bog down in a welter of details that couldn't possibly be associated with any story that had any point or ending. Finally the narrator himself bogs down and flounders hopelessly: "Now, where was I?" You no longer care where he was; you only care about where you would like to be—home. He has used a mountain of material to slay one mouse that might have really been a story.

But listen to a skilled raconteur. He knows exactly where he is going when he starts. If he brings in what appears to be divergence, you quickly discover that it is important to the matter. He excludes every word and phrase that does not lead directly to his ending. And mark this: he does not necessarily mind if you perceive the inevitable conclusion before he gets there. The most successful stage plays may not be those that keep the audience in the dark till the final curtain. On the contrary, if the audience begins to guess correctly the outcome, from that point they may be doubly gratified: they now have the pleasure of being clever enough to share in the art of working it out.

The interpreter who creates a whole, pares away all the obfuscating minor detail and drives straight toward the perfection of his story will find that his hearers are walking along with him—are companions on the march. At some certain point, it becomes their story as much as his.

It should be clear, from the foregoing, that while the interpreter is called upon to employ a combination of the arts, his main reliance will be upon a proficiency in what we call rhetoric; that is, the art of writing or speaking. Especially, it implies skill in the presentation of ideas, adapted to whatever situation is at hand.

CHAPTER V

Not Instruction But Provocation

The chief aim of Interpretation is not instruction, but provocation.

> The arts of education that will summon the people to learn are ... different from and greater than those which have been sufficient for the schools. . . . It is in fact powers of attraction in knowledge that are demanded for the new education. In the first place, attractive knowledge gains the learner and keeps him. In the second place it enlarges his genius, and out of that, his memory, whereas dry knowledge cultivates his memory at the expense of his mind. In the third place such knowledge is coherent with itself ... giving the learner a constant sensation that he is developing it for himself, which lets him into the legitimate delight of mental power.—James John Garth Wilkinson.

INSTRUCTION takes place where the primary purpose of the meeting between teacher and pupil is education. The classroom is the outstanding example of this, but it can apply to field and factory work as well. When, as early as 1899, college professors were beginning to take their students into areas that afterwards became national parks, their purpose was instruction. The students were not there primarily to look at scenery, to relax or to contemplate.

In the field of Interpretation, whether of the National Park System or other institutions, the activity is not instruction so much as what we may call provocation. It is true that the visitors to these preserves frequently desire straight information, which may be called instruction, and a good interpreter will always be able to teach when called upon. But the purpose of Interpretation is to stimulate the reader or hearer toward a desire to widen his horizon of interests and knowledge, and to gain an understanding of the greater truths that lie behind any statements of fact.

The national park or monument, the preserved battlefield, the historic restoration, the nature center in a public recreation spot, are exactly those places where Interpretation finds its ideal opportunity, for these are the places where firsthand experience with the objects of Nature's and Man's handiwork can be had.

Ansel F. Hall, then Chief Naturalist, delivered a message "to all park educational officers" in 1928, and I quote it here because it early made clear something that was afterwards misunderstood by many interpreters—that neither the function nor the aim of our interpretation is instruction:

In most Park educational activities it is best to give the visitor a broad, general idea of the Park in which he finds himself, allowing him to supplement the general but inclusive story with details according to his personal impressions of the facts which he himself gathers out-of-doors. He may gather these perhaps with your assistance, but he must be stimulated first to *want* to discover things for himself, and second, to *see and understand* the things at which he looks. . . . Remember always that visitors come to see the Park itself and its superb natural phenomena, and that the museum, lectures, and guided trips afield are but means of helping the visitor to understand and enjoy these phenomena more thoroughly. . . . A few believe it is our duty to tell as many facts as possible, and therefore take pains to identify almost every tree, flower and bird encountered. Others have taken as their motto "to be nature minded is more important than to be nature wise," and feel that it is more important that the visitor carry away with him an intense enjoyment of what he has seen, even though he has not accumulated many facts. . . .

As Ralph Waldo Emerson had written many years before, "Truly speaking, it is not instruction but provocation that I can receive from another soul."

In a book upon the principles of Interpretation it would be not only ungenerous, but actually a deficiency, to fail to consider the brilliant and unselfish efforts of the group of men that launched the educational program which, to a considerable degree, still remains the essence of National Park Service interpretation. Far from being an afterthought, the National Park Service was born with this ideal of employing the beauty and wonder of the parks, and the leisure that permitted visitation, as a sylvan path toward reverence and understanding.

It seems to have been a clear policy in the mind of Stephen T. Mather when he became the first director. As one of his earliest steps in implementing this policy, he persuaded Mr. and Mrs. C. M. Goethe, of Sacramento, to transfer to Yosemite National Park the venture in nature guidance that they had helped initiate earlier at Lake Tahoe. Their interest in such activity had been aroused after observing similar activities in their travels abroad. Mr. Mather gave warm encouragement also to Jesse Nusbaum's early interpretive activities at Mesa Verde.

Unfortunately there is not room here to recount all the fine spadework done in Interpretation between 1916 and 1928. Following these early activities, the Secretary of the Interior appointed a committee to make a thorough study of educational possibilities in the national parks, the expenses of the survey to be met by a donation from the Laura Spelman Rockefeller Memorial Fund. This group, consisting of John C. Merriam, Hermon C. Bumpus, Harold C. Bryant, Vernon Kellogg and Frank R. Oastler, went into the field and produced a preliminary report full of practical suggestions for "promoting the educational and inspirational aspects of the Parks."

During the following year three others, Clark Wissler, Wallace W. Atwood and Isaiah Bowman, were added to the first group, constituting an Educational Advisory Board to the National Park Service; and in ensuing years more field investigations were conducted in the parks and monuments. The final report pointed out "responsibilities and opportunities for education and research in the fields of history, earth sciences and life sciences," and laid down a program.

The early part of the background of Interpretation in the Na-

Visitors have the opportunity to view and understand the process of sand-cast moulding through an interpretive demonstration in the cast house at Hopewell Village National Historic Site, Pa.

Living history programs sometimes include the interpretive demonstrations of appropriate firearms. Morristown National Historical Park, New Jersey.

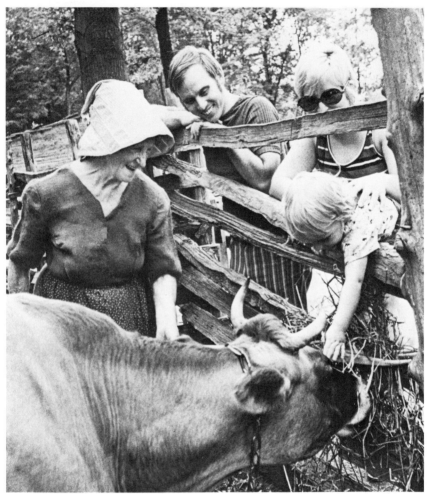

To help visitors gain insights into life as it was lived on the frontier during the early nineteenth century, Lincoln Boyhood National Memorial in Indiana uses a living historical farm.

*Visitors discuss Civil War military life with an interpreter in
authentic period dress at Petersburg National Battlefield, Virginia,
site of the last major battle of the Civil War.*

Demonstrations of routine daily chores from earlier times, by authentically dressed interpreter, are a basic component of living-history programs. Both the candle-making demonstration at Hopewell Village National Historic Site in Pennsylvania and the Colonial Kitchen operation at George Washington Birthplace National Monument in Virginia use smell and touch, as well as sight, to help enhance visitor understandings.

tional Park System has been summarized in a booklet, "Research and Education in the National Parks," by Dr. Harold C. Bryant and Dr. Wallace W. Atwood, Jr. (1932), and in "The History and Status of Interpretive Work in National Parks," by Dr. Carl P. Russell (1939). I wish that these papers might be available to interpreters generally, because they do so much more than the mere narration of the early work in this field. Personally I agree with the suggestion in the Park Service Administrative Manual that "Research and Interpretation" would best express the aim.

Finally, in 1953, as part of a reorganization plan for the National Park Service, with a view to strengthening the work of Interpretation in the field, a new division was created in the Washington Office, with a Chief of Interpretation directing and coordinating the work of the Branches of History, Natural History, Information and Museums. In addition, each of the five regional offices has its interpretation chief with a staff including a naturalist, an historian, a biologist and an archeologist.

With the giving of this brief background of the constant movement toward a more coherent and understanding program for Interpretation in the National Park System, I shall now look back a little upon the thoughts and feelings of the early workers in the field. Naturally these educators were concerned primarily with the educational possibilities in the scenic and scientific parks and monuments; in later years the System was to be augmented by the addition of a great number of historic and prehistoric monuments, variously designated, but all presenting chapters in the American Story. However, if I am correct in assuming that there is a philosophy of Interpretation, and basic principles upon which adequate interpretation can be built, the nature of what is being shown and illumined makes no difference. Interpretation is Interpretation anywhere, anytime.

The title of the booklet that emerged from the labors of the early educators, "Research and Education," was, strangely enough, misleading. Neither research nor instruction is of itself Interpretation. Yet each of the men involved in the survey was perfectly conscious that the desirable end was what we are now calling Interpretation.

Again and again in their individual reports they expressed thoughts which clearly showed that they had a keen sense of an underlying philosophy. I have no question that Merriam or Bumpus, for instance, if they had chosen, could have stated the principles of Interpretation with clarity.

The explanation is this: The members of the committee were bent upon formulating a plan for educational endeavor in the parks that could be put into some sort of practice at the earliest possible moment. They were aiming to fill what they considered, and Stephen Mather considered, a lamentable void. They pointed at that which could be readily understood in the field by field men. The enunciation of a body of basic principles could wait.

The plan was sound and admirable. It was comprehended, in its import, by many in the field. But others were unduly impressed by the word "education." The word, coming from well-known educators, suggested direct and detailed instruction. Thus, in so many cases that we have observed, the provocation to the visitor to search out meanings for himself, and join in the expedition like a fellow discoverer, was sometimes submerged in a high tide of facts, perfectly accurate, perfectly ineffectual.

My experience is that the groups of people who seek out interpretation in the areas of the National Park System are wonderfully well-mannered and pathetically eager for guidance toward the larger aspects of things that lead toward wisdom and toward the consolations that come from a sense of living in a natural world and a historic continuity that "make sense." And as a participant in such groups I have so many times had my enthusiasm wilted by an interlocutor who mistook information for interpretation—who became a poor instructor when he could have been an inspiring guide.

But mark how Dr. Merriam understood it. Consider these paragraphs from him:

The wider the range of observation and of thought on the part of the visitor, the greater the opportunity for what Henry Van Dyke described as "being lifted up through wonder into joy."

.   .   .   .   .   .

The mind of the adult requires more certain foundations in reality; it demands a clear exposition of relationships and definition of perspective.

.   .   .   .   .   .

There is danger that we study only the stones, that were left from parts of the buildings of the Maya, forgetting that they represent a people still living in the region.

.   .   .   .   .   .

There comes to me the story recently told by a friend who went out into one of those most remote corners of the Navajo Reservation to a place that some of you have seen in the Canyon de Chelly; that is, the White House. He was not able to go up this magnificent canyon because the sand was too deep. So they rode on horses along the edge of that magnificent cliff, with its roseate rocks that reflect the light of the sun in a most extraordinary way, and finally they came out on a high point. There they looked across the sandy wash to the eight-hundred-foot cliff on the other side, in the bottom of which in those great recesses were these magnificent buildings of ancient times known as the White House. And they stood there for a long time looking at this perfectly magnificent work, with the background of nature behind it. And then a Navajo came out from a little side canyon and stood on a rock in front of the White House and sang a song; and my friend said: "From the whole of my experience in that long trip this was the most magnificent thing—the story of man, with the great background of geology behind it, and then the expression of a living being illustrating the thought and the life of the people." And I said, "Why was that so wonderful to you?" And he thought a while and said, "I do not know."

Well, let us see if we can give the answer. Was it not, very simply, that the act of the Indian gave life to a picture that was otherwise beautiful but inert because it was unrelated to anything within the experience of the beholder? Was this not a fine instance of accidental interpretation?

Not the least of the fruits of adequate interpretation is the certainty that it leads directly toward the very preservation of the treasure itself, whether it be a national park, a prehistoric ruin, an historic battlefield or a precious monument of our wise and heroic ancestors. Indeed, such a result may be the most important end of our interpretation, for what we cannot protect we are destined to lose. I find in the Park Service Administrative Manual a concise and profound statement, and my heartiest thanks go to whoever it was that phrased it: "Through interpretation, understanding; through understanding, appreciation; through appreciation, protection."

I would have every interpreter, everywhere, recite this to himself frequently almost like a canticle of praise to the Great Giver of all we have, for in the realest sense it is a suggestion of the religious spirit, the spiritual urge, the satisfaction of which must always be the finest end product of our preserved natural and manmade treasures.

He that understands will not wilfully deface, for when he truly understands, he knows that it is in some degree a part of himself. "I do not wish to fling stones at my beautiful mother [nature]," said Emerson, "nor soil my gentle nest. I only wish to indicate the true position of Nature in regard to man, wherein to establish Man, all right education tends." It must be a bold person who would dare to amend our greatest American philosopher and interpreter, but I must dare it just this once. It is clear that Emerson was so intent upon the perfection of man that (for the moment) he failed to realize that Nature and Man are inseparable companions: They are one. If you vandalize a beautiful thing, you vandalize yourself. And this is what true interpretation can inject into the consciousness.

But not with the mere recitation of facts. Not with the names of things, but by exposing the soul of things—those truths that lie behind what you are showing your visitor. Nor yet by sermonizing; nor yet by lecturing; not by instruction but by provocation.

Not long ago I was one of a caravan that made a trip through one of the national parks. The leader, the interpreter, was a seasonal ranger, a college professor from another part of the country, who had been returning to this park for several years because he loved it. In the course of three and one-half hours (too long) this ranger took his group from one place to another. It was a hot day, and I was by turns amused and chagrined by his method—if it was a method. He violated almost every accepted rule of technique in dealing with his group. He horrified me by dealing largely in Latin taxonomy. Yet in the course of that hot and dusty trip the tired feet of the visitors stayed with him, and I began to see why it was. It was love. This seasonal man loved passionately every manifestation he was showing and describing; he transmitted that love and translated it to understanding.

Finally, standing upon the top of a bald mountain, this man gave me the last surprise. As fresh as though we had just started our tour, he told a thrilling story of the way the rock under our feet was attacked by the physical and organic forces; how vegetation begins; the creation of little harboring places in the rocks; the coming of grasses, of shrubs, finally of trees. Our grasses, our forests. The tired crowd followed with rapt attention. Then suddenly, after pointing out the centuries upon centuries that it takes to create such verdure and such beauty, he concluded abruptly, with a gesture and snap of the fingers: "And with a lighted cigarette *you* can destroy it all—LIKE THAT!"

Dramatized? Yes. Overdramatized? No. It was perfect. Not all the warning signs about fires ever put on the roadsides; not all the statistics ever published; not all the logic ever spoken, could have had the effect that this ranger secured upon his group. I say his group, because admittedly the occasion, in conservation, was special. We do not often have that chance.

But the point remains. It was not instruction. It was provocation.

CHAPTER VI

Toward a Perfect Whole

Interpretation should aim to present a whole rather than a part, and must address itself to the whole man rather than any phase.

> Wisdom is not a knowledge of many things, but the perception of the underlying unity of seemingly unrelated facts.—John Burnet, on Herakleitos of Ephesos.

OF ALL THE WORDS in our English language, none is more beautiful and significant than the word "whole." In the beginning it meant "healthy." I believe the thought it expressed was that no human being could be healthy who was well only in certain parts of his physical and moral self. "They that be whole need not a physician." (Matt. 9:12.) I believe there is not one of us who, looking back upon the errors of his own life, can escape the conviction that most of these were caused by mistaking a part for a whole. It is easy to do, for the contemplation of a part supplies an enjoyment of the understanding, while the search for the whole is hard work. "I see it all," we are inclined to say, when the fact is that we have not perceived the truth at all.

A cardinal purpose of Interpretation, it seems to me, is to present a whole rather than a part, no matter how interesting the specific part may be. It will be observed that I say "a" whole, not "the" whole. "The" whole soars into infinity, and the time we can spend with our listener or reader is all too brief. A friend of mine said to me, "The tourist has three limitations—of time, of absorptive capacity, and of money." Truly: so it becomes the more important to make of his contact an appreciation of a whole rather than of any part.

Imagine yourself in the presence of a visitor from some other planet. He has heard of a bird, but he has never seen one. You know a great deal about birds. You will perhaps want to tell him that the wing of a bird, in anatomy, is very much like the arm of a man, or the front leg of a horse, or that it even has its counterpart in a fish. Then the bird, as insect eater, is a friend of the farmer; and as food some of the birds are much sought by hunters. You could tell him a hundred interesting facts about birds, ending with that lovely artistic concept of John Ruskin, that "the bird is little more than a drift of air brought into form by plumes." Your visitor would be left wondering what a bird was like. A bird is a small whole, not an assembly of parts and attributes. If you don't think this is true, I beg you to take your parts and attributes and make me a bird.

At first glance, when I speak of a perfect whole, it may seem that I am indulging in a counsel of perfection—something extremely difficult for the interpreter to achieve. I believe the contrary to be true. It is exactly when, in an address to a group, the repeated interpretation tends to deal with a collection of discrete facts that both the audience and the interpreter himself become bored and listless. We all view with horror the possibility of what we call a stereotyped performance. Such a cliché is almost impossible when the interpreter has, either by intuition or by plan, managed to convey a dramatic whole.

Since intuition cannot be generally trusted, it follows that the interpreter must proceed from a principle, and the principle is this: It is far better that the visitor to a preserved area, natural, historic or prehistoric, should leave with one or more whole pictures in his mind, than with a mélange of information that leaves him in doubt as to the essence of the place, and even in doubt as to why the area has been preserved at all. To illustrate what I mean, I shall give an example derived from each type of preserved area mentioned.

First, from a primitive region, whether set aside for its beauty or its scientific qualities, or for both: Big Bend National Park. This is a desert-mountain-river wilderness, redeemed from a certain amount of former commercial use, and intended, so far as visitor access and accommodation may permit, to revert to its natural condition. Here a great dissected mountain mass of igneous rocks rises out of a plain that slopes toward the Rio Grande. Seen from the viewpoint of naturalist, historian and archeologist, there are thousands of interesting facts that can be told about what has happened here.

One of the stories here is the desert story. The spacing of the creosote and cactus growth in the lower lands is noticeable. The giant daggers are unique and impressive. The lovely agaves march up the sides of the Chisos Basin and burst into their swan song of flower at the age when they will sacrifice themselves for their species. There is a weeping juniper in the mountains that exists only in this Texas region, so far as North America is concerned. The highest peaks are forested with trees that you would expect to find much farther north in latitude.

What, then, among so many features that cannot possibly be absorbed in a tourist visit, may be a *whole* that would stir the imagination, leave an indelible impression, and lead the visitor to wish to know more about the subtle adaptations of organic life? What you see here is a story of diminishing rainfall, or rather, of precipitation. There has been a "flight" from increasing aridity over the many centuries. If you, the visitor, have come here from a region that receives forty inches of rain and snow a year, this is what, in general aspects, your land would look like, and the way the organic life would be forced to behave, if the rain clouds became reluctant. I do not promote this particular whole. The spot interpreter can judge better than I can. I merely say it is a whole.

Let us go to Vicksburg National Military Park. This Civil War shrine has great natural beauty, since it rests upon the deep fertile loess of the Mississippi bank. But presumably the visitor is here because of the dramatic long siege that resulted in the surrender of the city to Grant on Independence Day in 1863. This was one of the most involved operations of the war. If the interpreter were to have hours with his hearers, instead of minutes, he could not possibly exhaust the details of the manifold and fruitless attempts that were made to capture the stronghold from the river side. Grant's finally successful investment from the land side covers an

An interpretive wayside exhibit helps recreate the past at Yorktown in Colonial National Historic Park.

A model of Fort Sumter aids a ranger historian giving an orientation talk at the National Monument.

National Park Service stonemasons took apart weak sections of Hawaii's Great Wall, at City of Refuge National Historical Park, and rebuilt them to original standards to save the structure from further deterioration.

Meticulous research is an important prerequisite to interpretation of the slab-lined homes of pre-Columbian basket-makers of Weatherill Mesa in Mesa Verde National Park.

Human burials and artifacts discovered on the floor of a pit room in Mesa Verde National Park are carefully studied for what they reveal of a pre-Columbian culture.

almost equally involved series of military successes for the Union.

Here, again, there are wholes of far more meaning to the present-day visitor than the military strategy and tactics. A whole is found in the story of Missouri, as revealed in this siege and capture. The 11th Missouri regiment, USA, was on one side of the fighting; the 3d Missouri, CSA, was on the other. From that fact is illumined the human tragedy that was the War itself: fratricide. It reveals the story of a divided border state, with an animosity almost exceeding that of deep South and North. What difference does it make now, except to the researcher, who commanded these regiments? Or whether they were stationed on the left or right? Some of these Missouri boys, now striving to kill each other, were once fed gingerbread and doughnuts from the same Aunt Nellie's jar. That is a whole. Likewise the stark tragedy of Pemberton—the apostate Northern man who threw in his fortunes with the Southern cause, and became the very general who was forced to surrender the bastion—is a whole.

I happened to be at one of the smaller Southwestern monuments, Tonto, not far from the Roosevelt Dam in Arizona. While I was talking with the ranger-naturalist there he said to me, apropos of nothing in particular, "You know, Mr. Tilden, most of the people who come here look at that steep hillside up which the Indians climbed when they came back from their fields, and think life must have been a great hardship for those people. But I think they lived the life of Riley!"

I replied, "That seems to me a whole. I hope you'll weave that into a picture for the visitor who doesn't care whether the pottery was white on black or black on white, or who is not greatly exercised as to whether the migration into America came across the Bering Strait or by rafts to South America."

Of course, these prehistoric folk at Tonto had their ill moments, like people anywhere else. But at best it must have been a habitation of great pleasure, with few wants, the bright Arizona sky over them, and no hurry. The visitor himself, similarly placed and conditioned, would have done exactly everything these people did, perforce in almost the identical way, and he would have loved it, and thought his home the center of the earth, his children the best children, his gods the best gods. This is a whole, and though we owe such a debt of gratitude to the patient study of the archeologist, he must always remember that his tools are not the public's tools, nor his scholarly thoughts their thoughts. Hear what our Concord sage said of this:

> All inquiry into antiquity is the desire to do away with this wild, savage and preposterous There and Then, and introduce in its place the Here and Now. Belzoni digs and measures in the mummy-pits and pyramids of Thebes, until he can see the end of the difference between the monstrous work and himself. When he has satisfied himself . . . that it was made by such a person as he, and to the ends to which he himself should also have worked, the problem is solved.

Samuel Whittemore Boggs, the geographer, once spoke of "the wholesomeness of wholeness." When I first considered the statement, I was inclined to think the phrasing a bit overstrained. I now understand that Boggs was profoundly accurate. The wisest man is insufficiently conscious of the remedial quality of mere presence in the wilderness when he first comes from the marketplace of nerve-wracking half-truths and no-truths into a genial haven of a whole. Then as the jaded and shredded man senses the unmarred fabric of life all around him, he begins to feel himself becoming whole again. This is a phase of that "wholesomeness."

It is the same if he visits the scene of Washington's birthplace on Pope's Creek in tidewater Virginia. The house he enters is not the house where George Washington was born, but the spirit of our great whole man is there; and in these lovely and provoking surroundings, the staunch character of our hero comes to the imagination. Out of related and even unimportant facts emerges, at the instance of true interpretation, that greater truth, that all-important image—the character of the undaunted leader of the Revolution. The visitor takes hold upon himself. What Washington was in great, I can at least be in my little. These were the virtues of a whole man. I can safely aspire to be a whole man, too, though I am no Washington. It was this that Boggs called wholesomeness and wholeness.

For this and similar reasons the interpreter, whether in wilderness places or in historic houses or in the museum, must always make his appeal to the whole man that the visitor represents. This may seem contradictory, since in numberless instances the visitor could not well explain why he is present at all. But if you are to guess to what part-man you, as custodian, are to cater, the case is hopeless. If, for instance, you look upon him as a seeker of information upon some subject you specialize in, you are considering him in part, and that part, at the moment, may want nothing of your wares.

But if you make your target a whole man who seeks new experience, relaxation, adventure, imitation of friends who have told him "you mustn't miss it," curiosity, information, affirmation, and one thousand-odd other motives, you cannot fail to hit. He may be there for the explicit hope that you will reveal to him why he is there. I once remarked to a friend that we of the National Park Service are in somewhat the position of a wise waiter in a country hotel. Seeing that his guest is utterly bewildered by the bill-of-fare, the wise waiter does not directly propose a dish. He knows that the answer would be a rebellious "Don't want it." So he takes a subtle approach. "I noticed, out in the kitchen, that the chef has a very tasty stew today. It smells fine. I'm going to try it myself, when I get time to eat." Oftentimes the guest decides that this stew was exactly what he wanted, but just hadn't realized it.

Continuing the homely analogy, one thing leads to another. The guest feels comfortable after dinner. He thinks this is a pretty good hotel. Why not stay overnight? He has nothing particular to do. He takes a walk. The trees and the shrubs are greening with onleaping spring. He hasn't realized the beauty and the joy of walking for a long time. It's a better place than he thought; he is now conscious of the fact that there are a lot of interesting things to do here. . . .

It is unnecessary to elaborate further. The point is that the visitor was a whole man, not merely a human mechanism looking for something to eat and then go. And a whole man has moods. If for the moment he wants nothing more, in a primitive park, than to lie under a tree and look up through the green into blue, that is part of the whole man—a temporary mood. Do not disturb him.

He will be looking for something else later, and the custodians of these preservations set an ample table.

All interpreters, standing ready to serve the mood of the whole man, should cultivate humility. Not mock humility; that would be dreadful. But the true humility of one that is justly proud of his attainments, glad that it has been his fortunate lot to have a good measure of special knowledge, but infinitely patient with those who have not steered by such a constant star. It is good to remember that were you in the visitor's own bailiwick, you might be a stumbler. I am not sermonizing. I am suggesting good and understanding interpretation.

I have myself heard visitors to parks and historic monuments and museums ask some ludicrous questions. It is easy to put the visitor down as a moron. Often, however, I have been certain that these silly questions arose from a genial desire on the part of a visitor to say something so as to assure the interpreter that he was appreciative of the discourse. There not being time to consider, a stupidity resulted. Let the talk turn to something the visitor already knows: he will say nothing foolish.

Dr. Clark Wissler said, "Every ranger has the tendency to overestimate the background the tourist brings to the scene and on the other hand to underestimate the intelligence of the 'average visitor.'" I do not think this is as true today as when Dr. Wissler noted it; but adequate interpretation will not make this mistake.

Mr. Emerson wrote: "And there are patient naturalists, but they freeze their subject under the wintry light of the understanding." Emerson had just as much admiration of the "patient naturalist" as any man. He meant simply that "the understanding" is only one of the attributes of a whole man. His natural religious spirit, his emotions, his yearning for continuity, his love of a story, his physical pleasures are among other parts of him that must be considered.

CHAPTER VII

For the Younger Mind

Interpretation addressed to children (say, up to the age of twelve) should not be a dilution of the presentation to adults, but should follow a fundamentally different approach. To be at its best it will require a separate program.

> To the young mind everything is individual, stands by itself.... Later remote things cohere and flower out from one stem.—Emerson.

M R. EMERSON was thinking, I believe, when he wrote the word "later," of a maturity of men and women when they can begin to grapple more or less successfully with abstractions. Then, indeed, "remote things flower from one stem." But Mr. Emerson would be delighted, were he here, to observe the splendid interpretive work now being done for children—the nature centers, the museum exhibits, the trail walks and talks, and all the rest—for it was not done in Emerson's day. There were the textbooks, and there was the teacher, and there were the more or less obedient pupils; and perhaps it is the best tribute to those devoted teachers to say that they were able to lay some of the educational dust that settled over the classroom where firsthand contact with the objects of study was not usually available and often not even encouraged.

If Mr. Emerson could visit an area or two of National Capital Parks, or the Cook County Forest Preserve District, or Colonial Williamsburg, Cooperstown, Old Sturbridge or Greenfield Village—to name a few places of brilliant achievement in interpretation for children—he would agree that skillful guides are making "remote things cohere" not later, but now.

Let me give an instance. Not long ago I heard a naturalist speaking to several hundred grade-school children. In the course of his talks he used the word "ecology" several times. When I was a schoolboy we should have called that a hard word. We called any word ending in "ology" a hard word. I realize now that hard words are exactly those that represent things we are not prepared to be interested in. The naturalist had previously explained to these children that the word signified a life community of grasses and trees, of insects and birds, of rodents and reptiles, whose fortunes were bound together in their "home" place. The children were not merely interested, they were fascinated by this idea and its connotations. So the word ecology was an easy word, besides being a rather showy addition to their stock of nouns. But the point is that the concept of this association of living things, replacing a classified list of creatures all going it on their very own, is surely a coherence of remote things achieved while these children are still children.

These same children would probably complain that the words "sociology" and "theology" are hard words. They are just not yet prepared to be interested in these implications.

Considering the brilliant success of so many nature centers, museums (whether called by the name or not) and other activities of interpretation for children, I should suppose that my sixth principle will find general acceptance, considered as a principle. Naturally there will be many views as to the methods or techniques employed. It is true, too, that the most effective programs for children will, at present, be in locations most accessible for arranged visits of school groups. These are, at the present, mostly areas of day-visit, though a preserve like Colonial Williamsburg is able to supply accommodations for a longer stay.

There also arises the question of cost and staffing for the maintenance of children's programs. As to this, all I would say here is that on reviewing the work now being done by the larger institutions I am sure that there is no preserve so small that it cannot employ some devices, if it desires to do interpretation at all. Few places can ever do the job as handsomely as Williamsburg, but any historic house or humble museum can use some of the basic ideas in a relatively inexpensive way.

The selection of an upper age limit of twelve years, as stated in this principle, sounds arbitrary, and is in fact so by intent. It will not be misunderstood, I am sure. Very important factors of interpretation for children continue their validity into adolescence and maturity. Reading matter, oral presentation and other media aimed at the intermediate school level has been definitely found to interest older children and even adults.

The earliest school years find children learning the names of things at a phenomenal rate, never again matched. It is the period when we do not tire them by giving them factual information as such. The interpreter who has dealt with both young children and adults will have noted the eagerness for pure information in the one and a slight aversion to it in the other. This difference of itself suggests that interpretation for children implies a fundamentally different approach.

Surely certain characteristics of young children are carried over, with more or less diminished intensity, into the later years. One of these, of somewhat humorous aspects, is the delight in the superlative. I have followed a group of kindergarten children in a museum where some of the adventurous thrill obviously came from holding in the hand "the biggest egg" (ostrich) and "the littlest egg" (hummingbird's in nest) and from seeing the skeleton of "the biggest animal" (whale) suspended from the ceiling. There was an heroic-sized statue at one end of a room. Every child, I observed, touched this statue in passing it. I asked the interpreter-teacher why they did so. "Because it is so big. They would not have patted a statue merely life size." In a section devoted to wildfowl eggs, the attention was arrested and held by one collection of two dozen together. "It was the biggest lot," was the explanation.

Does this love of the superlative sound childlike? Yes, until you recall that several million adults spoke with great relish of the "biggest blizzard" (1888), and that other millions enjoy such superlatives as: the highest mountain in the world (Everest; though, in fact, there are several peaks in the Himalayas only a few feet less high); the biggest petrified saurian ever found; the proximity of the highest and lowest point in the United States proper (Mt. Whitney and the below-sea-level extreme in Death Valley); the first robin seen in spring; the smallest church—multiply these instances as you will.

Another characteristic very pronounced in younger children, partly because of their lack of inhibitions, but carrying over in no little degree through life, is the love of personal examination through three senses other than sight and hearing. Most notable is the urge to know "what it feels like." Interpretation in the past has failed to make full use of the opportunities for satisfying this tactile urge, and at present interpretation for children is making much more use of the experience than is that for adults. The naturalists, perhaps, have the best chance to employ the smell and taste experiences, and some of them do it very effectively. At the door of the Little Red Schoolhouse in the Cook County Forest Preserve, I saw a small bag hanging from a nail; the label underneath read something like "Smell it. What is it?" Without a second thought I reached for it and sniffed the herb that was within. My own act was instinctive.

"What does it smell like?" It is an educational experience that goes beyond the mere odor of the object itself; it takes the child or the adult into fields of like or associated odors. An odor memory is cultivated or renewed. Children who live in rural places come to know very early by both taste and smell a large number of plant species—even the qualities of various clays—but as the country becomes more and more urbanized, there are more and more millions who can get such acquaintance and knowledge only from public preserves where interpretation is done.

Quite aside from education, the knowledge of an experience with odors is now seen as so important in the field of interpretation that when I was in Cooperstown there was a discussion of some method by which the old Tavern could be given an authoritative tavern odor—a consideration that seemed to me just as important in bringing past into present as providing an historic structure with the furniture of the period. For it is part of the same aim: to give the visitor a sense of living the very experience of the ancestor.

In Cooperstown Farmers' Museum I was struck by the great number of pieces relating to rural life of the period from the

Revolution to about 1850 that can be touched and handled by children and adults. Indeed, I think Dr. Louis C. Jones, the Director, rather proudly told me that they had only one object that children had to be kept from, and that was because of danger of injury not to the object but to the children. Incidentally, because of this free use of touch, I wondered whether there was not considerable loss by accidental breakage or vandalism. The Director said that on the contrary, such loss or repair in the previous year had been almost nil. His theory about vandalism, by the way, is worth considering. He feels that the high caliber of an exhibit, plus a warm feeling that the visitor is welcome as a guest, furnish a restraining influence. I believe that there are other considerations, but these two are certainly of high importance.

Not only are young children willing and eager to absorb a great number of factual statements as such, but we observe, once the fact is accepted, how meticulous they are that the fact should not suffer from tampering. I recall once reciting to a little three-year-old, at her request, the true-and-tried "Night Before Christmas." She had heard this many times and knew it by heart. When I came to the lines "When what to my wondering eyes should appear, but a miniature sleigh and eight tiny reindeer," a spirit of mischief prompted me to say "*seven* tiny reindeer." The little lass glared at me as though I had uttered a blasphemy. She said in firm rebuke, "*Eight* tiny reindeer!" The adult would have passed it as an unimportant slip, not really caring whether Santa had eight or twelve. Perhaps this is what Emerson meant by saying that "to the young mind everything...stands by itself." It may also underline the necessity of patient research as a prerequisite to preparation of literature and other media for children, so that the facts will indeed be facts. However, from what I have seen of the competency of our interpreters, there is no danger from this viewpoint. More important is the truth that has been constantly impressed upon me: interpretation for children, as a branch of art, requires a very special talent.

Many writers of ability in literature for adults has failed miserably in the attempt to do books for children. I am myself a good illustration of the fact, for I once wrote a juvenile at the invitation of a publisher, the result of which effort failed to beguile even my own children, though for reasons of family loyalty they made vast pretension of being delighted. I shall leave it to others to explain precisely what this talent connotes. I have seen much of it in action and am still puzzled.

Not long ago I heard a young naturalist giving a slide talk at the newly created Rock Creek Nature Center of National Capital Parks. The old stone house formerly known as the Klingle Mansion had recently been converted into a delightful repository of exhibits and work-it-yourself devices pertaining to the natural world. There are many objects here that can be touched and handled. On this particular occasion the teachers had been invited to choose the subject. Geology, which they chose, is not an easy subject to communicate to either children or adults. But never were children more obviously given the spirit of adventure than on this occasion. Afterward I asked the naturalist if the fact that he was pretty young himself—about twenty-five—had anything to do with his success with the children. He considered, and finally said he thought not. No doubt he was right, for I have heard much older interpreters, including a college professor in his fifties, similarly adroit with child groups. Of one thing I am certain: one factor of the general talent is the ability to give the sense of companionship and conceal any show of direct instruction. Not that children resent such instruction in the classroom, but these visits to places of firsthand experience are different. Here the story becomes more important; here the adventure factor is uppermost. I suppose this is the reason why Greenfield Village has a film-strip of pre-visit orientation called "A Museum is a Story," both to emphasize an alluring fact and also to take a supposed curse off the word "museum." Yet I doubt if children are as much frightened of that word as adults are generally supposed to be.

Albert Manucy, for many years the historian at the Castillo de San Marcos in Saint Augustine, asked me, "Have you considered the ability a child possesses to identify himself with the historical scene?" Indeed I have, and among other places in Albert's own fine area. I have wondered whether this facility does not arise in the first place from the child's great ability to see. We know too well that

The Dinosaur Quarry Visitor Center is a unique building constructed against the face of a fossil-bearing cliff. Dinosaur National Monument.

Skilled excavators expose fossil bones of extinct giant reptiles on the cliff that forms an interior wall of the visitor center.

Careful research on the excavated cliff face is part of the preparation for interpretation.

In Wupatki National Monument three generations of one family inspect ruins of prehistoric Indian apartment houses, with the aid of a ranger archeologist.

the adult fancies he sees much when he really has seen little. Anyone who has taken a walk with a feverishly active boy of eleven years and returned limp from merely being asked to "look at that" will realize what I mean.

Now, at the Castillo de San Marcos, there used to be in the sally port a small bronze cannon pointing inward toward the parade ground. Seldom did a group of children visit the fort that one or more of them failed to ask, "What's it pointing that way for? The enemy would have come from the other direction." I never heard a similar remark from an adult. And it was usually children who showed puzzlement concerning the unmounted cannon on the fort roof: "How could they fire them?" Of course, in a matter like that we must realize that children are not usually afraid to ask questions, and many adults are, from fear of saying the wrong thing.

Further to capitalize upon this ability of the child to associate himself with the scene, some institutions are now supplying the schools with pre-visit material: orientation folders, descriptive literature, film-strips on loan, and other matter designed for the intermediate grades or for older students, or for both. Colonial Williamsburg, which has entered this field in a large way, says that "teachers have found that students using advance briefing material have a better learning experience in Williamsburg." It could hardly be otherwise. Though such a program as Williamsburg's is expensive to maintain, I shall again point out that even small and understaffed and underendowed preserves can do *something* of the sort. I venture the statement that any museum, historic place or other institution that attempts to bring past into present will eventually succeed or dawdle to precisely the degree it manages to interpret effectively for children. If we cannot interest with our treasures those carefree young persons whose minds are at the height of receptivity, how can we hope to interest those adults who are inevitably fogged and beset by the personal and social worries of an uneasy world?

In this chapter I have attempted to do little more than to give personal observations of interpretation for children that seemed to support the view that the principle involved is truly a principle, and that it is being most effectively activated by many institutions and by interpreters. Nothing that I have noted should be taken as hinting that I have proficiency in child psychology, which indeed I have not. I reiterate that I am convinced that interpretation for children requires a very special aptitude, though this does not mean that certain persons may not have talent to conduct programs for both children and adults, or even for those most difficult visitors, the adolescents, who have in the past few years been marked and treated—as I believe most unfairly—as being almost a distinct species of the genus Homo.

Also, I should add that though I have mentioned but a few of the admirable programs currently conducted, I have chosen these with no thought of being discriminatory. All around us amazingly fine work in interpretation for children is going on. Besides, my reports of institutions that I have not been able to visit, and my accumulation of their bulletins, brochures, quiz sheets and the like, have been vastly encouraging. Finally, to applaud the rapid increase and the excellence of this effort is not to depreciate the constant improvement of interpretation aimed at the adult.

PART
TWO

CHAPTER VIII

The Written Word

A spade is not sharpened by being called a
geotome.—Norman D. Newell.

THIS CHAPTER does not offer a course in the writing of interpretive signs, markers, labels or printed literature. It presents thoughts and examples consonant with the principles stated in the first part of the book.

I feel sure that some day there will be a school with regular sessions held successively in at least four regions of the United States, where those of the National Park Service, and members of other agencies concerned with the graphic phases of interpretation, will meet to compare experiences, discuss examples, present their own productions for discussion and assay, and listen to at least one talk by a selected person who has made notable progress in this difficult field of expression. Whoever gives this talk will certainly be one who sincerely admits that he himself is still a patient student. The intricacies of this branch of art make it certain that no one person will ever be its complete master.

To begin a little discursively, I will note the fact that many years ago, being enamored of the challenge of Interpretation, I set myself the task of collecting and studying what we may refer to as the "inscription." This specifically includes relatively brief messages, indoors or without, aiming at something deeper than mere information.

I began with Greek epigraphy. I confess that I never reaped any great harvest there, for the Greek inscription was primarily, by intent, a tiny jewel of poetry, even when comic. One thing, however, makes this ancient artistic form worth our attention: the success in making a few words tell a full and moving story. The celebrated epigram of Simonides (any English translation can but feebly capture its original elegance) engraved on a monument at Thermopylae, is worth mentioning:

> Go tell the Spartans, thou that passest by,
> That here, obedient to their laws, we lie.

The couplet expressed to the Greek wayfarer as much as pages of history text could have. No wonder he wept when he read it.

One more quotation from classical inscription will suffice. If you happened to know that St. Paul's cathedral in London was designed by Sir Christopher Wren, you would naturally expect to see there either a blunt announcement of that fact or a statue of the architect. What you see is a laconic inscription: "Si monumentum requiris, circumspice." (If it is my memorial you are looking for, gaze around you.)

A tablet of five hundred words recounting the achievements of Wren would be feeble compared with that understatement.

First, we should consider what place inscriptions of the several kinds occupy in the scheme of the interpretation of an area. That they constitute a rock bottom there can be no doubt. Some millions of visitors are going to receive their first—and many will unfortunately get their only—impressions from this source. Especially in an area set aside for its scientific values, a sign employing technical and unfamiliar language may serve to chill the interest in the whole. If he cannot readily understand the interpretive sign or label, the visitor may easily conclude that the place is a little beyond his normal capacity to enjoy.

A directional sign may be scrawled with red chalk on a shingle and prove to be better than none: it serves to give information that is of first importance. This is not true with the interpretive marker. I have noted many cases where a blundering marker was worse than nothing at all. Consider this one, not actually used, but suggested for a spot near the salt pools in Death Valley. It begins: "The remnant of ancient ice-age Lake Manly maintains its water level from 4 to several feet beneath the uppermost salt layers. . . ."

What is the visitor unskilled in geology—particularly the regional geology—to think of that? This sign accosts him with the ice age, of which he certainly has only the vaguest notion, and with Lake Manly, nonexistent now except underneath the salt, of which he cannot be expected to know anything. Death Valley is said to be the "paradise of the geologist." It can be the wonderland of the non-geologist, too, but not if you start with an introduction like that.

I recall a case of objects in a museum in the South, where war materials of the Civil War period are displayed. The label refers to the pistols and other objects as "artifacts." Truly, since they were made by man, they are artifacts. But they are relics, aren't they? Isn't that what we commonly call them? Why call them by a name that makes the visitor think he is facing something obscure?

Such examples as these take us directly to what I shall now discuss, which is the frame of mind and the basic considerations from which a good inscription must spring. The creation of the written interpretive work—and it is equally true, of course, of the preparation of oral material—is a matter of two stages: thinking and composition. Of these two, it must be apparent that the first is the more important. If the thinking is sound and the composition halting, the result will never be entirely bad. On the other hand, if the thinking is poor, even if the writing is brilliant, the result is worthless or even mischievous. Except for the rare instances of inspiration, I should guess that the adequate interpretive inscription will be the result of ninety per cent thinking and ten per cent composition. Inspiration is usually the mirrored reflection of hard work.

THINKING

Probably the most common error in creating interpretive matter of all kinds derives from the fact that the writer has in mind the question: "What is it I wish to say?" It is of no importance whatever, as yet, what I wish to say. I have not reached that point. The important thing is: What would the prospective reader wish to read? And what can I say in brief, inspiring and luring terms about this area in language that he will readily comprehend?

For myself, I have found in the writing of inscriptions that it is of great advantage to have in mind some person of my acquaintance and write straight to him. In the days when I was doing much public speaking, I found it useful (and other speakers have told me the same thing) to pick out some cheerful inviting countenance in the audience and mainly direct my words to her or to him. It develops a conversational as opposed to a starched-shirt manner.

It seems hardly necessary to say that the preliminary thinking is dominated by a love of the subject in hand, plus an active interest in people. Axiom: Whatever is written without enthusiasm will be read without interest.

It is highly necessary to visualize the encounter between your message and the visitors. It is useful to the writer to be familiar with the exact spot where the inscription will be placed, but this is not absolutely necessary. Again, it is a great help if one can know of certain spots where almost invariably the visitors ask one leading question, as at Badwater, in Death Valley.

But more important is to have answered for yourself, as interpreter, the vital questions: "What is the keynote of this whole place? What is the over-all reason why it should have been preserved?" It is for this reason that I have in time past suggested what I call the "master-marker" which would be, as one might say, the title of the book, and the rest of the markers would be chapter heads. Not every area would lend itself to this scheme; in some the master-marker would be the only marker. As to where such a master-marker would be placed, the administrator of the area should best know. In some cases, headquarters would be the favorable location; in others, the place of largest congregation. But certainly neither the master-marker, nor indeed any inscription, should intrude itself between visitor and the object intended to delight and impress. And there are spots where no interpretive sign should be erected. Nature, and even artifice, can sometimes speak for itself better than the interpreter can. Personally, I should not ever wish to see a marker exactly upon the bald summit of Cadillac, in Acadia National Park.

Sometimes a quotation will be found more effective than anything we can currently invent, to project the right mood into the mind of a reader. The Minute-Man inscription on the boulder at Lexington Green may be taken as an example:

*Interpreters can lead visitors to vistas of great beauty; appreciation
must come from within. Longs Peak from near Trail Ridge Road,
Rocky Mountain National Park.*

Campfires go back to man's early beginnings. An interpreter at Grand Teton National Park discusses the activities of the day with a group of campers.

The stillness of a primeval time is preserved in the redwood forests of Muir Woods in northern California. Research provides interpretation with an interesting story of these living fossils.

Sometimes the underground world can seem alien to us. At Timpanogos Cave National Monument, an interpreter accepts the challenge of helping visitors relate to an unfamiliar part of nature.

Line of the Minute-Men
April 19, 1775
Stand Your Ground
Don't Fire unless Fired Upon
But if They Mean to Have a War
Let it Begin Here
—Captain Parker

Can you imagine anything we can now say of the outbreak of the
Revolutionary War that would be better than this?

Or, at the lovely Brookgreen Gardens in South Carolina, where
the Huntingtons established and endowed the largest outdoor
museum of sculpture in the world, in the shade of the live oaks you
are greeted with this quotation from the canticle of St. Francis of
Assisi:

> Praised be thou, my Lord, with all thy creatures,
> Especially the honored Brother Sun,
> Who makes the day and illumines us through thee
> And he is beautiful and radiant with great splendor;
> Bears the signification of thee, Most High One.

In reading a life of Alexander von Humboldt recently I came
upon a quotation that might be effectively used in these days of fear
and frustration: "Let those who are wearied with the clash of
warring nations . . . turn their attention to the silent life of vegetation . . . and remember that the earth continues to teem with new
life."

That sentence heartened me, somehow, and I feel sure that if I
had stumbled upon it in one of our many quiet woodland or
meadow retreats I should have thrown back my shoulders and
taken on a touch of renewed confidence. So, as interpreter I ask
myself, "Why should not others get the same result, since I am
just one of the crowd?"

Still, as to quotations, we must consider that in spite of the fact
that thousands of fine things have been said, worthy of preservation
in print, it is really uncommon to find one that exactly fits the needs

we are discussing. And of course it is only too human, when one is stymied in the sweating-out of a good sign, to seek a quotation as the easy way out.

One of the choicest signs I know is that by Bob Mann, in the Forest Preserve District of Cook County, Illinois:

> I am an Old Time Country Lane
> Now I have been
> Officially Vacated and Closed
> (I never liked automobiles anyway)
> I invite you to walk—as folks
> have walked for generations
> and be friendly with my trees
> my flowers and my wild creatures.

What an invitation that sign is to the tired, restless, perplexed and jaded soul! Bob wrote to me humorously that the sign was composed "mit beer." I don't care whether it was dashed off on the spur of the moment, or laboriously wrought. What I do know—and we are talking at this moment not of composition but of thinking—is that it could not have been born of anything but years of sheer affection for and understanding of nature and people, and the needs of people.

Perhaps this brief comment will serve to point out the indispensibility of deep meditation of all the conditions to be met, of the subject and of people and their limitations, before any writing whatever is attempted. I suppose it sums up this way: You must be in love with your material, and you must be in tune with your fellow man. What ensues is composition; not easy, needing pitiless editing and cool criticism, full of pitfalls, barbed with discouraging false starts and notes—but a great joy when the bullseye is hit. But the thinking will determine the result.

COMPOSITION

The chief thing that makes the wording of good inscriptions so exacting is the requirement of brevity. "Anybody can write a novel," said a famous magazine editor to me one day, "but there are few good short-story writers." While this was a deliberate exaggeration, for not everyone *can* write an acceptable novel, the statement was based upon an important truth.

Interpretive signs, museum labels, and the like will be usually read by standing people. There are exceptions, such as when a drive-off permits people to remain in an automobile and read. People are not conditioned, save perhaps for straphanging commuters, to much reading while standing. I found in Blue Ridge Parkway, at the entrance to a self-guiding trail, a large glass-covered case that contained, in hand-lettered capital letters, several hundred words of the best writing I had seen in a long time. It was salty, neatly turned, with the homeliness of the mountains and mountain people. It delighted me. But I observed that visitors merely gave it a glance and turned away. It was too long, and it was in capital letters. Except for headlines, readers are not conditioned to "caps." They read them under eye protest.

Brevity, of course, is to be taken comparatively. What would be sufficiently laconic in one circumstance would be too long in another. Generally speaking, an area of day-visitation will require briefer inscriptions than one where people feel a greater sense of leisure. I concluded after a stay in Death Valley that interpretive signs could be somewhat longer there (if the subject so indicated) than in most of the park system areas.

Three kinds of brevity defeat their purpose. One is the sort called telegraphic, where articles "a" and "the" and even words are omitted. I have just looked at an expensively executed bronze plaque, otherwise satisfactory, which was ruined by this bad writing and bad taste. Another is the kind where, in striving for brevity, the sign fails to convey an adequate message. Much as we desire to avoid unnecessary wordage, reasonable latitude in length must be allowed. The third case is really an error in preliminary thinking, rather than in composition. A sign may include a statement that requires an explanation, but for brevity's sake the explanation is omitted. An illustration of this I saw at Montezuma Castle. A sign there says that "Montezuma is a misnomer." (*Misnomer* is a fancy word for *wrongly named*. It is not in common use.) It is true that Montezuma the Inca had nothing to do with this area, but you here read something that is meaningless unless explained. The answer probably is that it need not have been mentioned at all. It is the sort of information that may well fit into a folder or handbook, where it can be properly handled.

Ronald Lee handed me this inscription, which he saw in the Southwest:

> A Building Stood Here Before 1680.
> It was Wrecked in
> The Great Indian Uprising.
> This House Incorporates
> What Remains.

This is brief, and I judge from what I know of the building, entirely adequate.

Here is an example of a brevity that makes for inertness and failure to capture interest, when the addition of a few words would create an interesting mental picture:

> This Rock
> Marks the Spot
> Where
> Daniel Webster
> Spoke
> To About 15000 People
> at
> The Whig Convention
> July 7 and 8 1840
> Erected by the Stratton Mountain Club

It was not a convention in the present political-party sense, but that is not the serious error in the inscription. The point is that the sign is dead when it could be very much alive, for this political rally of 1840 was actually an amazing thing. Let us see if we can make it move. Daniel Webster began his speech on this occasion with the words: "From above the clouds, I address you...." So, as his opening words create at once the picture of a great crowd being on a high mountain, why not begin with the quotation?

"From Above the Clouds I Address You...."
Daniel Webster
Statesman and Orator
Spoke Here
to 15000 people
Who had Come in Farm Wagons
In Carriages
and Afoot
To the Rally
For "Tippecanoe" Harrison
For President
in July 1840.

Aside from the fact that few persons now know what a Whig was, while most people have heard of William Henry Harrison, the inscription now has movement. It was no small thing for fifteen thousand people to toil up a high mountain to hear oratory. They took their politics seriously in those days!

Wherever this element of movement in a sign is possible, it is most effective. Here is a sample from the New Hampshire State Preserve at Franconia Notch:

The Basin
Over a period of centuries
a pothole was formed by the
action of a large stone
turning and *spinning*
under the pressure of *rushing*
whirling water, in a depression
of the granite stream-bed.

The italics in the above are of course mine. They are legitimate words that graphically describe how the pothole was formed, and I do not think the use of four participles for this purpose was over-doing it.

Movement may be suggested by a picture. On U.S. Route 24 through Ute Pass at Divide there is a sign: "Yonder is Cripple

Creek." Underneath is a miner with his burro, and under that: "World's Greatest Gold Camp." The picture furnishes the sense of motion.

HUMOR

We now arrive at one of the touchiest qualities of inscriptional writing—humor. At the outset we can all agree that its use should be with discretion, finesse and fitness. Humor out of place is a sad excrescence. Humor in harmony with the thing, and the mood, is a charm to most people. What is humor? Thackeray thought it was "a mixture of love and wit." Wit alone is often biting and unkind. Humor, especially that of the turn of phrase, or the oddity of conceit, brings a contented smile. In Bob Mann's old-time country lane sign, the line "I never liked automobiles anyway" is a flash of humor. Bob makes the old lane speak its mind and gives it a personality.

The Montana highway signs that have cheered everyone who has driven the roads of that state have many touches of true humor. They thus distinguish these inscriptions and earn a national comment. In the old days, says one of these signs, "you rode a saddle horse to get places. Some people wish it were still like that." Here is a nice dab of the nostalgic that appeals to us all; for enmeshed as we are in the mechanical web, we all yearn for an hour with mud pies and oxen.

"There are people," said Emerson in an essay on "Culture," "who can never understand a trope, or any second or expanded sense given to your words, or any humor; but remain literalists after hearing music and poetry and rhetoric and wit, of seventy years. They are past the help of surgeon or clergy."

You think of Emerson as a learned philosopher and hardly expect to hear him say anything funny. Nor does he say anything *funny*. But if there is any more delicate sally of humor that makes you bubble joyously in your inwards than the paragraph about the pale scholar with bent brow and firm intent, who goes out into his garden to get "a juster statement of his thought," finds himself pulling weeds and ends by being "duped by a dandelion"—I know not where to find it. (Essay on "Wealth.")

Inscriptional matter should be written generally with lightness but never with levity. Get that clear distinction in your mind, and you save yourself from what is slangily called the corny. It is the light touch that brings the sunshine out of the cloud. As an example I present an inscription on a monument at Quebec, honoring both Montcalm and Wolfe: "Valor gave them a common death, history a common fame and posterity a common monument."

Here is a noble subject, nobly approached; but observe that unlike many a heavy-handed and lugubrious treatment, it has the lightness of touch that, in this case, happens to be part of the genius of the French tongue (this quotation being a translation). I admit that this whole subject is a difficult one. It is one of those things about language that either you feel or you do not. If you do not see the shades of difference between the heavy and the light attack, you are not as yet equipped to write inscriptional matter.

I suggest the following inscription for some desert spot, where a welcome *remada* is surrounded by desert plants. There is no warrant herein for the slightest humor. We wish to tell a story and give a warning. But the touch is light:

> The desert is a severe mother, bent more on justice
> than on mercy. Through generations of survival these
> plants around you have found means of protecting
> themselves from death by heat and drouth. Note the
> varied ways. You, too, must learn the wisdom of
> the desert if you would be safe within it.

When you are able to write with a light touch, without indulging in humor, then you shall be permitted to write humor with a light touch. That, to me, sums up the matter.

CHAPTER IX

Past into Present

> He held it always as a maxim, that History did
> greatly serve . . . to the ordering of a man's life.
> For he counted it as, in certain ways, more
> effectual than Philosophy, which indeed in-
> structs men with words; but History thrills
> them with examples and makes them partakers
> of things and times which are past.—Gassendi,
> *Life of Peiresc.*

ALTHOUGH none of the wilderness preserves are without some
historical associations, this chapter will primarily concern
itself with the prehistoric and historic areas of the National Park
System, and of the many other shrines, publicly and privately
owned and administered, where the effort is made by interpreters
to turn back the pages of time and establish a vital relationship
between the visitor and the memorialized people and events.

As to the primitive parks, however, this much may be said: that
of all the millions of visitors to them, the fullest appreciation of
unspoiled nature is found by those who are willing to imitate in
some degree the experiences of the pioneers, even though it be
actually a pale partaking, devoid of most of the hardships and
dangers. Campers, certainly, rather than cruisers of the roads; yet
only those campers who are willing to leave the spots of congregation and strike into the back country may be said truly to partici-
pate. We shall look closely at this rather baffling word "partici-
pate" in the following pages. Even if the valiant few who taste the
joys of absolute self-reliant freedom of the wilderness are not
condemned to live off the land as the mountain men and French

voyageurs did, they return home with a keen perception of the rigors that faced the pioneer.

Visiting the places that have been made famous and treasurable by the acts of men and women, where the story is told of courage and self-sacrifice, of dauntless patriotism, of statesmanship and inventive genius, of folkways, of husbandry or of the clash of armed men following their ideals to the valley of the shadow—all this offers a very different kind of experience. These places may be physically beautiful, and they may exemplify artisanship of the highest order, and furnishings of the most exquisite taste; but whether they are those things, or whether they are humble log cabins, rudely equipped, in a bleak environment, they all point to the same thing—they represent the life and acts of people. Consequently, the interpreter will endeavor, if he is presenting an historic house, to "people" that house. Architecture and furnishings are much; we admire and draw conclusions from them, but we must find the art to keep them from seeming to have been frozen at a moment of time when nobody was at home.

The prehistoric ruin must somehow manage to convey the notion to the visitor that the ancients who lived there might come back this very night and renew possession, and that there will be a renewal of the grinding of corn, the cries of children, and the making of love and feasting. This must not be taken too literally. I am trying to project a possible feeling. The battlefield of our great fratricidal American war is not merely a place of strategy and tactics; not a place where regiments moved this way and that like checkers on the board; not merely a spot where something was decided that would lead to another decision. It is a place of the thoughts and acts of men, of their ideals and memories; a place where on the evening of a fatal tomorrow men could joke and sing; a place of people, not armies. For we Americans are not descendants of a regiment; we are sprung from men and women.

If you go into that charming Adams house in Quincy, Massachusetts, you see a home that was occupied by several generations of one of our most extraordinary families—rugged individualists, if there ever were any; intellectuals, unspectacular, nonconformists. In Oregon is the home of John McLoughlin, "father of the

Oregon Territory," another rugged individualist, but how different from the Adamses! At Hyde Park there are the homes of Vanderbilt and Roosevelt, each representing a sharply-etched way of life in a period of our history. But wherever, and whatever, in the places devoted to human history the objective of interpretation remains unchanged: to bring to the eye and understanding of the visitor not just a house, a ruin, or a battlefield, but a house of living people, a prehistoric ruin of real folks, a battlefield where men were only incidentally—even if importantly—in uniform. I was thrilled once at the sight of a picture of a poor ragged fragment of a defeated Confederate band, straggling past an officer standing on a hillock by the side of the road, and bravely managing a salute out of their remaining morale. Hardly a whole uniform among them! I said to myself, "*This* was the war."

I shall not elaborate further on this. All understanding interpreters know as well as I what the ideal interpretation implies: re-creation of the past, and kinship with it. The problem is how to achieve this desirable end. It is not easy. It is quite the contrary. There are hundreds of physical difficulties in the way of letting the visitor and the thing indulge in a desirable intimacy. Objects are often fragile, and many structures cannot bear indiscriminate use. The vandal is dreaded. There are many irreplaceable treasures. No generalization as to management will hold, for what could be tolerated or encouraged in one place would be speedily fatal to another. So, in interpretive effort we are constantly considering ways and means of bringing the past to the present, for the stimulation of our visitors, as local conditions may permit. Two of the devices frequently discussed in the field of Interpretation are demonstration and participation. We shall look at those, and it may be that we can add a third.

DEMONSTRATION

Dr. John Merriam once quoted with great relish a characteristic instance in the Middle Ages of depending upon theory and description, when a simple demonstration would have resolved all difficulties at once. There was a spirited discussion among a group of scientific men over the nature and number of teeth possessed by a

*A park naturalist shows a family how to quietly observe wildlife, in
this case a cow moose at Isle Royale National Park.*

A guided walk in Yellowstone.

At an overlook in Bryce Canyon National Park.

Evening Campfire programs are excellent opportunities to present the geological and ecological backgrounds for daytime interpretation of the Bryce Canyon National Park's features.

horse. Literature was quoted, authority was marshalled, and the discussion was raging ineffectively when somebody abruptly suggested that they go out and get a horse.

Demonstration is the act of "bringing in the horse." You may write pages or talk interminably to me about the process of grinding flour and meal between stones revolved by a wheel driven by the flow of a stream, and I shall still be too little aware of what actually takes place. After seeing the operation in process at Mabry's Mill on the Blue Ridge Parkway, at Rock Creek Park in Washington, or at Spring Mill State Park in Indiana, my curiosity is satisfied. We must remember that our country has become so greatly urbanized that there are now millions of adults and children who have never seen a cow milked.

The Steel Institute has reconstructed, on its original site and in the most faithful replica, the first successful ironworks in America. On the Saugus River, in Massachusetts, at stated intervals (because the water must be used sparingly) the visitor may see not merely the physical equipment and structures, but the movement of the machinery of the rolling and slitting mill. At the fine Farmers' Museum at Cooperstown, thousands of delighted visitors watch the old-time process of breaking flax, of weaving, and of candle-making; and to make the demonstration even more impressive, a little plot of soil shows, nearby, flax plants in growth.

On the top of the Castillo de San Marcos in St. Augustine, the visitor sees some ancient cannon, lying on the roof with muzzles pointing ineffectively through the ports. It is obvious that something is missing in the picture. It is necessary to explain that these supine implements, in their present position, could not be used at all. When I was last at the fine old Spanish fort, the superintendent was trying to get funds that would mount a few such guns on carriages, with the necessary equipment to demonstrate how they were actually used. A demonstration, most illuminating, could show the whole procedure up to the moment of actual firing.

Again, at this Castillo de San Marcos, there is a provocative instance of how demonstration can be turned into participation, and thus obtain both elements at once. For many years the guides at the fort have paused at the doorway of one of its storerooms, which in the early Spanish days was secured by an ingenious three-way lock. The leader of the tour never failed to interest his group when he demonstrated exactly how the locking-up was done. One day an experiment was tried. After his demonstration the ranger invited one of his group, "Come and do it yourself." The effect was clearly stimulating. Though the participation was immediately that of only one person, the rest of the group somehow felt that *they* were helping to do it. An unexpected by-product of this simple expedient was told to me by one of the guides. He said, "That demonstration at the doorway seems also to have the effect of pulling my group closer to me all the rest of the tour."

One of the most ingenious devices of demonstration I have seen was in the Desert Museum in Phoenix, Arizona. The peculiar methods by which desert plants resist the terrific dehydration of the torrid summers are familiar matters of descriptive talks and literature. But, choosing the great saguaro cactus as an example, some good thinker in interpretation has partly exposed the root system of a living plant and affixed a thermometer that demonstrated how the plant keeps its internal temperature constantly below the heat of the air. This is most effective demonstration, and while it seems of a very special kind and opportunity, I have not the least doubt that we could find in our primitive areas many related chances.

Once, in Big Bend National Park, I had Natt Dodge take for me a color slide of a Mexican laborer standing in a clump of lechuguilla plants. Over his shoulder is carried a bag of the sort the natives have for centuries woven (as well as ropes, bridles and dozens of other things) from this very plant. Among our most effective efforts at interpretation are the demonstrations of how not only aboriginal people but our own pioneers used the material that they found at hand to create the things they had to have. A demonstration of the actual processing of the lechuguilla would have been, of course, even better; but that, like so many other opportunities that must be reluctantly passed up, meets administrative difficulties.

I could go from here to a long list of excellent demonstrations that are actually being done either in National Park Service areas or by other interpretive agencies, but the point I wish to make is that we have by no means more than skimmed the surface of the possibilities in demonstration. That demonstrations will never be sufficiently numerous in any place of interpretation I sadly admit. No doubt local peculiarities often forbid them. It must be added, too, that lack of money and personnel have prevented, in the past, such desirable development of this fruitful educational device. Still, I am persuaded that in many areas much can be done with little, if imaginative and deliberate assessment of the possibilities is employed.

Finally, the word "demonstration" and its implication are readily understood by all those engaged in interpretation. It would be fine if we could say as much of the commonly used partner word:

PARTICIPATION

Here is another term in Interpretation which, like the very word "interpretation" itself, needs a reasonably well-accepted definition. I say reasonably, because it has already become clear to me that we interpreters are never going to agree precisely upon the point where "participation" begins to be of sufficient weight to merit the term. What we can all agree upon without reservation is that the thing we mean by the word is of the utmost importance in enlivening the visitor's sense of, and feeling for, the past in natural and human history. To argue about the definition of the word is farthest from my purpose. My feeling simply is that we should have, when we use any word, a fairly general tacit acceptance.

The dictionary will not help you. It is another of those words to which interpretive activities have given a special significance. The only thing that will help is the discussion of examples, ranging from what we all, without dissent, admit as participation, through examples which will be disputed, and finally down to instances where most of us will feel that the word ceases to have any significance at all.

To me, it is elementary that participation, in our sphere of interpretation, must be physical. When you try to make it include what is wholly or predominantly mental, the word is stretched beyond meaning. Not only must it imply a physical act, it must also be something that the participant himself would regard as, for him, novel, special and important. I cannot believe that a man who eats hasty pudding and codfish balls really thinks that he is participating in the life of the provincial Boston of Cotton Mather; on the other hand, I am quite sure that when he takes the barge ride on the old C&O canal, in our National Capital Parks, he feels the distinct pleasure of reverting to a period that has long gone. He sees the mules tugging at the towrope, and passing through the locks can easily imagine himself a traveler to Cumberland, taking his ease on deck and greeting his neighbors at the halting places.

On the contrary, the group headed by a Supreme Court justice that walked the C&O canal a few years ago were not participating. It was a good and amusing stunt, but the canal was a means of common carriage in its heyday, and about the only pedestrians were the mule skinners.

The carriage rides at Williamsburg, as I see it, come gracefully within the meaning of our term. Yet these have not quite the degree of true participation that John D. Rockefeller, Jr., with fine imagination, planned for Acadia National Park when he created the carriage roads that were to give a taste of the horse-and-buggy days and a leisurely savouring of the joys of driving a lovely countryside, with ample opportunity of viewing unspoiled natural scenes. Alas! the horse became too nearly extinct, and liveries too expensive, before the plan could ripen its humane fruit.

Nobody would question a high degree of true participation in the days when visitors could climb the ladders to the cliff dwellings at Montezuma Castle in Arizona, a vivid experience that had to be written off when it became clear that the fragile ruins could not endure the heavy visitation. But the rutted roadways over which the pioneers of the Oregon migration passed are still available, and so are the bypassed stretches of trail that diverge at many points from the Parkway of the Natchez Trace. At Pipestone National Monument I suppose it would be possible to obtain a pipe of the identical catlinite from which for centuries the Indians made their calumets. The pipe could be filled with the "kinnikinnick" or inner bark of the dogwood that still grows abundantly, thus affording anyone, with the curiosity to do it, the identical material for true participation.

I was at Death Valley National Monument one day, gazing at

the famous well of the Bennett-Arcane Party of 1849, when a family arrived at the spot in an automobile. One of the party, a girl of about fifteen, came over to the pool with a tin cup, leaned as far out as possible, scooped up some of the water and drank it with gusto. I had the impression, though she did not say so, that it was a deliberate act of participation on her part. At any rate, I so considered it.

Not because of any close relationship to the participation offered in our areas, but because it seems to me to point to an acme of true participation from which we can determine the validity of various shades of meaning of the word, I include here an experience mentioned in a current scientific magazine. Two Danish archeologists, curious about the aboriginal use of the stone axe in felling trees, as well as the subsequent burning and planting of such a cleared area (the primitive practice in agriculture), engaged in a well-studied experiment. Using artifacts that had been dug from a swamp, they actually felled large trees, and burned and cleared and planted. They discovered exactly how the chopping was done, for they found that a stone axe freely swung, as we use a steel implement, broke or chipped under the force of the blow, whereas a short, pecking stroke did the work and did not injure the tool. Without describing this experiment further, it occurs to me that it was a classic of participation from beginning to end. (If you had been watching them in the course of their work, for you it would have been a demonstration.)

Visitors to our archeological areas would be certainly participating if they were to take a handful of corn grains and with mano and metate grind this corn to meal. I should like to see this opportunity generally afforded to the visitor. He would not necessarily have to use the ancient artifacts, for the Mexicans are currently manufacturing plenty of contemporary manos and metates for their own use. But I also know that these artifacts exist in great abundance all over the Southwest and it would take several centuries to use up the supply.

All in all, the opportunities for bringing to the visitor a journey into the past by means of participation will never be as abundant as we should like. The point I make is that participation and demonstration are such priceless ingredients of interpretation that we should diligently search for possibilities and never let slip a real opportunity for including them.

But there is another effective implement of interpretation that is clearly neither demonstration nor participation. I shall call it:

ANIMATION

If you do not happen to like the word "animation," perhaps you will prefer to call it "local color" or "atmosphere." I like the word animation to describe the thing, because to animate is to give life, to vivify. Again, the definition is not so important if we can agree on what the activity is, or can be.

On a Sunday afternoon I went to the Custis-Lee Mansion, "Arlington House," just across the Potomac from Washington. As I entered, somebody was playing the piano. It seemed so perfectly natural that somebody would be playing a piano in a house that had sheltered the Custises and the Lees, or indeed in any historic house where people had lived! I had been many times in this famous home and had delighted in its beautiful maintenance. I had, in truth, never actually felt it to be cold; but like so many other precious relics of the past, its treasures have to be safeguarded, and most of the rooms can be seen only from their doorways. That is a penalty we must pay for preservation.

But now, I felt that this house was peopled. Not by visitors like myself, but by those who had best right there—the men and women who loved the place because it was home. In a drawing room an attractive girl, costumed in the period of 1860, was playing the very tunes that were current at that time. It could have been a neighbor lass of Miss Mary Custis at the instrument, which itself was of the very period. There was nothing obtrusive about the music, and I noted with pleasure that most of the visitors were not curious about it, a sure sign that it was in perfect harmony and accepted as part of the re-creation.

On one occasion there was a "St. Patrick's Day Celebration" at Arlington House. Now that is not in harmony, someone might say. But if they did so say, they would be ignorant of the fact that George Washington Parke Custis was noted for his sympathy with the Irish cause of freedom, in that day when it was a burning political question. He wrote an ode to "Young Ireland," gave many addresses on the subject, and threw himself into the ardent dispute with all his accustomed vigor. It *was* in harmony, this celebration, and it helped to people that mansion. It was animation.

I believe that many of the beautifully planned and executed devices at Colonial Williamsburg, aimed at bringing past into present for visitors, can properly be described as animation. But whether or not we wish to call them so, we should realize that effective opportunities for such interpretation lie all around us in our activities.

An enduring sense of the heritage from our fathers is vital to our future, and this knowledge is to be gained by keeping the past a living reality. *There* is strength. I remember talking one day with Ronald Lee about the pleasant feeling of participation I had had in walking portions of the old Oregon Trail in Western Nebraska and Wyoming. "But it is more than that," said Ronnie, speaking for himself as a Westerner. "To me it brings a sharp realization that the West is a part of our great Whole, and has its share in the general heritage. It gives us the thrill that we belong."

One of my favorite books is John Merriam's "The Living Past." * His title alone supplies us with an interpretative ideal.

* The experience described by Dr. Merriam at Canyon de Chelly, page 37, seems to me an ideal example of what I mean by animation.

CHAPTER X

Nothing in Excess

> Too much noise deafens us; too much light
> dazzles us; too much distance or too much
> proximity impedes vision; too much length or
> too much brevity of discourse obscures it; too
> much truth astonishes* us.—Blaise Pascal.

THE SAYING "nothing in excess" is attributed to several of the Greek "wise men," but in truth it is far older than that. It probably dates from the time when a primitive man tried to bolt too large a hunk of mammoth meat.

For myself I got a taste of this wholesome injunction years ago when I had a country house that needed wooden shingles. I hired an old cunning carpenter of the neighborhood to do the job, but then I was seized with the ambition to try my own hand at laying a square. The experienced eyes watched me for a few moments. Then he said, "Would ye take a little advice? The way you're doing, you'll split the shingles. Never give the nail *that last tap*."

Whenever I am visiting one of our preserved areas, whether a park or a museum or a historic house, and whenever I hear an oral interpretation or read a written one, I am sometimes reminded of that homely remark. There are so many instances where, injuriously and to the detriment of an otherwise fine presentation, the nail has been given "that last tap." The descriptive folder that does not end when enough has been said; the last twenty color slides that collapse the camel; the "one more last thought" of an earnest speaker who bulges with an enthusiasm wholly laudable; the museum that

---

* Astonish, in the old sense of "bewilder."

responds to the humane thought "we just can't leave that out"—all these excesses spring from admirable intentions. But the interpreter must survey his work from the point of view of the visitor, and take into consideration all the factors that make an audience restive, easily sidetracked, and too readily gorged, especially when it has little familiarity with the subject.

I recall one rather comic instance of the "last tap" in a certain museum filled with a display of highly specialized objects brought together by a manufacturer of fine cultural leanings. The museum is beautifully housed, free to the public, and is of such importance that the school authorities of the city make a visit to it a prescription for the children at some time during their study years.

Unfortunately, almost the very first thing the young visitors observe when they enter the first hall is a painting. The picture, to be sure, is by one of the old masters, and very fine. Nor is the subject alien to the objects on display. The difficulty is that the principal figure in the painting is a lady who, at the moment the artist saw her, was not wearing any clothes. She is very lovely, and there is no tinge of vulgarity in the art. But children are children, and high school pupils are adolescents, and the day I happened to be in the museum, a troop of young irrepressibles was gathered around the picture poking each other in the ribs and giggling. From that moment, the excellent exhibit was in grave danger of disappearing down the drain, speaking from the standpoint of education.

The answer is simple. The owner of the painting considered it fine art, and it is; he felt that it could be displayed with propriety, and it can; he was sure that it fitted with the general subject of the museum, and he was right; but he could not bear to leave it out, and he was wrong. It is excess. The display would be better off without it.

In Lafayette Square, in Washington, there is a statue of Kosciusko, the Pole who fought for American independence. Well he deserved a memorial in the capital city of the Nation. But the base of the statue bears the inscription, "Freedom shrieked as Kosciusko fell." Of course, freedom did nothing of the sort. Freedom never shrieks, however much it may honor, esteem or lament. It may be said that the quotation is from a poem of Thomas Campbell, "The Pleasures of Hope." In a whole poem and regarded as a bit of license, it may pass. But in an inscription it can be seen only as an error of excess. Inscriptions, particularly when dealing with noble subjects, should avoid words that produce undignified pictures.

In interpretive markers we should be chary of using words like "heroes." Certainly the men were heroes who are so described; but it is better to tell what they did, and the visitor will not forget that the acts were heroic. Indeed, when it occurs to him that it was heroism, it is borne in upon him more forcefully than if he were told so. "They fought against great odds, but they held their position." This sentence proves they were valiant, without using the word.

I say in another chapter that you do not make a scene more beautiful by calling it beautiful. In a sense, you make it a little less so. It is the same with excessive words. Let us cultivate the power that lies in understatement.

I find in my notes the following reference in quotes: "...that admirable restraint which springs from good taste and perfect understanding of the limitations of the subject." I do not know now whether I wrote this or whether I copied it somewhere. Anyway, it is to the point. Such poise is an indication that the interpreter feels deeply and thinks clearly about the essence of what he has in his custody.

Let us not fall into the humorous mistake of the florid exponent of "chamber of commerce" literature. It is self-defeating when issued to persons of judgment. If you tell me that your locality combines the grandeur of the Alps with the serenity of an English village, and the historical pageant of the Loire Valley with the mystery of Tibet, I reply that there is no such damned place, and if there were, I should avoid it; and I drop your folder into the wastebasket.

There are so many and such varied pitfalls in this matter of excess that I can here give but a hint of the general danger. Even this much I dislike to do, since I have planned the book almost wholly upon the side of affirmation and construction; but the devil is always at our elbow, suggesting that one last touch of virtuosity. When

One of the author's principles of interpretation is that interpretation is "revelation based upon information." Visitor center information desk, Great Smoky Mountains National Park.

National Park Service, M. Woodbridge Williams

Natural features that might otherwise not be understood by the visitor take on new meaning through interpretation, as with this glacial erratic in Acadia National Park.

Beauty, of and for itself, needs no interpretation. Later, questons will come. "What great natural forces lie behind all this?" Then the interpreter's moment has arrived. Looking into Yosemite Valley from Dewey Point.

color guide to wildflowers

These plants, arranged by flower color, grow in this region. Knowing them by name is the first step in learning about them.

Do-it-yourself interpretation. Pressed specimens in protective cases help visitors learn the names of plants of the Blue Ridge Parkway, Virginia–North Carolina.

in doubt, say "no." The world has never been much hurt by abstentions.

"Multiplication is vexation," the children of the McGuffey Reader period used to chant; and so it is, in a very different sense than they perceived. I say nothing here of the bewildering collections sometimes found in museums that have never had the services of those experts who know something of what museums should be. Gradually we are atttaining a high excellence in museum work. Still there is a tendency, even in some of the more modern institutions, to resort to quantity. I have always enjoyed a good laugh at the Florida animal farm which advertises 2,000 alligators. The alligator is an interesting reptile, and I imagine they are very fecund, so that as in the case of guinea pigs you may run up your stock pretty fast. But the menagerie in question pretends to be no more than a menagerie; it does not style itself a museum. When people are in a holiday mood, or want to break the monotony of a long automobile trip, it is quite possible that 2,000 alligators may be just the right number, and if the quantity should drop to 1,900 there would be great disappointment.

Yet, I had the alligators vividly recalled when I attended the Hall of Fame and Baseball Museum in Cooperstown, New York, and saw a tremendous number of autographed baseballs marshalled in cases. I am personally predisposed toward baseball; it is a fine sport. It is not for me to say whether it is a pastime of sufficient importance to justify the distinction here given it. I had a fancy, during my visit, that perhaps it might better form a section of a Museum of American Sports, in which all our games would be represented. But the point I make is that the mere multiplication of autographed baseballs does not increase the interest in the exhibit. I am on dangerous ground now, for the baseball *aficionado* is a hot-blooded fellow who has been known to threaten the umpire with bodily injury.

What I say of baseballs seems to me equally true of churns, trivets, Currier and Ives prints, coins, stamps, indentures or any other of thousands of items—unless, of course, the single purpose of the exhibit is to show such things as a specialty.

Another excess leads to diffusion of interest. The commonest example of this, in private life, is the agony suffered by the friends who have been invited to come over for the evening and see projected on the screen some of the pictures George and Alice have taken with their camera. They may be slides, or they may be motion strips. The lens has a most uncanny way of picking out for a beginner shooting his first color roll some of the best shots he is ever likely to achieve; but if George and Alice had edited their collection carefully the evening might have been more successful. All these pictures have equal merit in the eyes of the entertainers; the victims are rushed from a backyard cook-out to the seashore, from sister's baby to the petunias, from the birdbath to the autumnal colors of a maple tree. The result is a dizziness that cannot be traced to the cocktails. You have seen nothing because you have seen everything. This is the numbness of diffusion.

I give above an absurd and extreme instance in the domestic world. But some years ago I visited a very fine historic house, lovingly arranged and maintained. It had been the home of a famous author. Somewhere, during a journey abroad, the author had written a single comment: "This evening we all went to the circus." Based upon that single clue there was included among the exhibits a miniature circus. It was a very neat and charming little circus. But what possible place had it in the house? Had the author's youth been spent as a trapeze performer with Barnum, it would have been true to the biographical picture. This is diffusion.

A peculiar kind of excess in some of our scenic parks is the disposition to set up telescopes, usually operated by dropping money in a slot and serviced by a concessioner (when they are serviced at all, for frequently they are out of order and the coin is lost), with the purpose of bringing the distant objects nearer. In some cases, as when there is an extraordinary geological formation situated where it could not otherwise be seen by the visitor, such a device is clearly desirable. In general use, they minimize or defeat the opportunity to get that sweeping sense of magnificence that only the human eye, with its normal range and backed by imagination, can procure. What other reason was there for setting up this viewpoint, or developing this overlook, than that you should get

the full effect, rather than to distinguish rocks and trees as individuals?

The artist draughtsmen have a neat name for pictures that labor
in confusing detail. They describe them as being "too busy." I had
a friend who, though a most successful illustrator for the magazines, had always had a struggle to conquer his tendency to busy-
ness. One day when I was loafing in his studio he said to me, "You
know, I was wondering last night, just before I went to sleep, if I
were cast away on a desert island in the Pacific, and could bring
only one tool ashore with me, what tool I should prefer that one
to be."

"A knife?" I suggested, not too brightly.

"No," was the reply, "an eraser."

CHAPTER XI

The Mystery of Beauty

Doth perfect beauty stand in need of praise?
Nay; no more than law, no more than truth,
no more than loving kindness, nor than
modesty.—Marcus Aurelius, *Meditations.*

IN THE DOMAIN OF aesthetics, the interpreter must be wary. It is
not good to gild the lily. Not only is the lily destroyed, but the
painter has made a confession that he does not understand the nature
of beauty.

There is no adequate definition of beauty, though there are many
noble essays; and this is true, I believe, for the reason that beauty
is at once an abstraction and a reality. You might be interested
in the way Bernard Bosanquet interprets Plotinus on the subject:
"Beauty is all that symbolizes, in a form perceptible to the senses,
laws eternally active." Kant found that beauty (the sublime) is
"that which by its . . . mightiness shocks us and fills us with pain at
our own smallness, but then fills us with a feeling of the exaltation
of the greatness of our own nature."

Describe it how you will, it is certain that beauty is a very real
as well as an elusive thing, and it could be an element for the lack
of which the human being would not care to live.

For my purpose, and as a caution to the interpreter in the whole
field of aesthetics, I choose one of the best passages of Emerson:
"Nature never became a toy to a wise spirit. The flowers, the animals, the mountains, reflected the wisdom of his best hour, as much
as they had delighted the simplicity of his childhood."

In concrete example: If we are showing the majesty of the Teton
Range, we must not do or say anything that would make a toy of

this experience. These Alpine peaks know how to speak for themselves, and they speak a language that the world of people shares.

An object, whether a mountain, a lake, a crystal, a Chippendale or an heroic act, is not made more beautiful by being called beautiful. And the perception of beauty is always in the nature of a surprise. We sometimes humorously call overlooks in the National Park areas "ohs and ahs" from the fact that these exclamations are the spontaneous manner in which the visitor expresses his wonder-struck feeling. Thus, in an interpretive sign you are not wise to describe any definite object as beautiful; besides being impertinent by infringing upon the visitor's taste, you are interposing between him and the scene. But there is no harm in using a phrase like "the beauty that surrounds us in this region," for now you are establishing a mood, and the generalization, concerning which there would seldom be any disagreement, leaves the person a free choice as regards any single object.

So, I think where the interpreter is dealing with aesthetic values he will do well to restrict himself to two offices: first, to create the best possible vantage points from which beauty may be seen and comprehended; and second, to do all that discreetly may be done to establish a mood, or sympathetic atmosphere.

It may be, as Ronald Lee suggested to me, that this first endeavor is a principle of Interpretation. I do not reject the idea; it may well be. But since I think of it as so greatly a matter of design, management, planning, landscaping, road construction or whatever, I prefer to deal with it in the present manner. That it is a function of the highest importance there can be no doubt. Also, whatever may be said of the establishment of the vantage point and the mood for the contact with beauty may be said equally, though in varying degrees and by varied means, of the wilderness park, the museum or the historic house.

Specifically, then, wherever the major aspect of the thing is aesthetic, I would have no oral or written interpretation that did more than deftly create a feeling, and rather for the whole than for a part. For the rest, it is a study for the master planner and the landscape or other architect. Mr. John D. Rockefeller, Jr., with his sensitive eye for the surprise in the enjoyment of the natural scene, may err on the side of too many vistas, which, truly enough, can do some violence to the concept of unspoiled natural conditions; but I think his underlying purpose is sound and generous, both qualities characteristic of him.

We should not attempt to describe that which is only—or better—to be apprehended by feeling.

In South Carolina, the outdoor museum of sculpture called Brookgreen Gardens is the humane and artistic creation, on the site of an old plantation, of two splendid amateurs, the Huntingtons (a felicitous interpretive marker from these gardens is quoted in Chapter VIII). Here, as it seemed to me when I spent several happy hours there, is an instance of an institution that needs very little interpretation, oral or otherwise. There are some questions arising in the mind of the visitor, but these do not concern the aesthetic qualities and could well be answered (as perhaps they are since I was there) in a small leaflet. For the greatest part, Brookgreen Gardens is self-interpreting. The mood and the vantage ground are established in the very essence of the place.

But consider Craters of the Moon National Monument, near Arco, Idaho. Here is something that requires adept interpretation to be realized in its beauty and wonder. I say "beauty," for to me it is beautiful, since I follow John Ruskin in the thought that fitness is the first element of Beauty.* But if my neighbor thinks this hurly-burly of volcanic forms is ugly, I shall not argue. We merely define beauty for ourselves differently.

Craters of the Moon pictures Nature in agony. The magma could no longer be enchained; it boiled up from the depths and flowed out, and hurled itself upon the earth, cooling in astonishing forms. Since most people think of beauty as something perceivable through the eye alone, here is a challenge for the interpreter. He must take the visitor into that larger sphere of the same quality, which we may call order, or perfect compensation. His task, then, is to make a living and thrilling story of that marvelous balance main-

---

* "Can a dung-basket, then," said Aristippus, "be a beautiful thing?" "Yes, by Jupiter," returned Socrates, "and a golden shield may be an ugly thing, if the one be beautifully formed for its particular uses, and the other ill formed."—Xenophon's *Memorabilia*.

National Park Service, Jack Boucher

The elevated Anhinga Trail in the Everglades National Park serves three purposes: effective interpretation of an otherwise inaccessible environment, convenience to the visitor, and protection of a fragile wildlife community.

A National Park Service instructor prepares a group for exploration of the underwater wonders of Virgin Islands National Park.

Demonstrations of mountain industries and crafts are always effective interpretive media, as in this sorghum-cane grinding operation at Mabry Mill in the Blue Ridge Parkway, Virginia.

Visitors to Blue Ridge Parkway get to taste apple butter cooked in the old-fashioned way.

tained by Nature, whereby a loss of weight in earth structure at any given spot is restored at some other, maintaining the axis we currently enjoy.

Similarly, in a steep-walled canyon on which is written the drama of ages of erosion and deposit, though the major aspect is not commonly thought to be aesthetic, the beauty of it can be made to appear in this larger sense. I sometimes wonder whether almost all of what we are trying to interpret does not fall, at last, into this realm of the aesthetic, in- and out-of-doors. Following this thought, the sod house of the Dakota settlers becomes not merely a bit of social history, but something beautiful, because Man used to full purpose that which he found of the materials at hand. I once saw a structure in Big Bend National Park mostly built of the dry flower stalks of the agave and of ocotillo stems, roofed with rushes from the river bank. Was that not beautiful? It is when we resort to cunning inventions that we so often create the truly ugly.

I find the smithy, as seen in a number of our fine reconstructions of the village life of our past, a beautiful thing. Even the man himself, plying the bellows; the rich red that comes into what were almost dead coals; the sparks flying from under the hammer beat; the very simplicity of a muscular, fitly-clothed man using expertly the rudest tools in creative work—all this is not merely history, which would be fine in itself, bringing past into present with nostalgic sweetness, but deeper than all this: the reflection of Man's will to do, and his kinship with all that breathes around him, and even with the ore that sleeps in the ground, awaiting his touch.

All this the interpreter can project in simple terms, but only if he himself feels its beauty. Out of his special knowledge he can do much more, of course; but this feeling is elementary. From this, and out of his studies and his research, he molds all into a "single science" (as Socrates phrased it); and whether you wish to call this love, or beauty, or something you think less pretentious, the effect is to send the visitor away with something more than a fact, and we may call that something inspiration.

If I were arranging a museum, whether of minerals or other things, I think I should have the visitor see, as he enters, one beautiful, unlabeled thing. If it is surpassingly lovely of its sort, it is of no consequence, at the moment, what its specific name may be. Anyone who wishes to know later will be informed. I would have ample space around it, so that nothing could jostle for supremacy. I am not a museum expert, and if it were left to me to create a whole museum, I fear I should make sad work of it. But I do feel sure that I am right about establishing the mood and the stance.

Darwin was in Brazil as a scientist; but he spoke as a visitor when he wrote: "It is easy to specify the individual objects in these grand scenes; but it is not possible to give an adequate idea of the higher feelings of wonder, astonishment and devotion, which fill and elevate the mind."

If a man of science could so feel, then the finest uses of national parks, or indeed of any of the preserves that come within the range of interpretive work, lie ultimately in spiritual uplift. This end cannot be reached except through a walk with beauty of some aspect, in which the interpreter is not primarily a teacher, but a companion in the adventure.

CHAPTER XII

The Priceless Ingredient

> Like a great poet, Nature produces the great-
> est effects with the fewest materials—sun, trees,
> flowers, water and love; that is all. If, indeed
> the last is wanting in the heart of the beholder,
> the whole is likely to seem to him a daub; the
> sun is only so many miles in diameter, the trees
> are good for firewood, the flowers are classi-
> fied by the number of their stamens, and the
> water is—wet.—Heinrich Heine, *Die Harzreise.*

Henry James, in his very un-Jameslike book *A Little Tour in France*, gives a humorous description of the "interpretation" provided at the ancient Cité of Carcassonne, in Provence: "It was not to be denied that there was a relief in separating from our accomplished guide, whose manner of imparting information reminded me of the energetic process by which I have seen mineral waters bottled." After escaping from the guide, James "treated himself" to another walk around the citadel—alone.

We all know this guide as though he had fizzed in our presence. We have met his like—a little better, perhaps, but also perhaps a little worse. Such guides are not all in France. I am reminded of a party of visitors I joined to explore a limestone cave. The guide was amiable and personable, but he had made two major mistakes in the work he was pursuing—without catching. In the first place, he had committed a recital to memory, and he suffered a lapse of memory before he had got very far. This may be a source of embarrassment to the interpreter, but it is worse for his auditors, for they not merely bleed with him—they bleed for him. After that agonizing stoppage, our guide said, "Well, I'll begin again. . . ." This time he sailed through.

But the second defect was the fatal one. He had undertaken this interpretive work without being in love. If you love the thing you interpret, and love the people who come to enjoy it, you need commit nothing to memory. For, if you love the thing, you not only have taken the pains to understand it to the limit of your capacity, but you also feel its special beauty in the general richness of life's beauty. This, to be sure, may make you tend to over-emphasize your particular task; but the fault is corrected as you come to know more about the limits of time, absorptive abilities and a just proportion.

Before going farther, I must explain definitely what I mean by a "love of people." Precisely I do not imply any mushy view of humankind, or an exaggerated notion of their virtues. In the course of a long career, the interpreter will meet the pestiferous, the un-manageable, the ineducable, and some whose apparent reason for existence is to provide the hangman with work. These are not the many; they are the few. One who has suffered a number of attacks by poison ivy may get the idea that this malicious plant dominates the scenery. In truth it occupies only a little space in the whole floral luxuriance.

The interpreter will not abase himself, he will insist upon being treated with respect, and he will have no taint of mock humility. He will be humble, not because he is overawed by his contacts, but only because he falls short, in his own judgment, of the flying perfect at which he aims.

No, indeed; you are not to love people in any sickly sense. You are to love people in the sense that you never cease trying to under-stand them and to realize that whatever faults they have, whatever levity, whatever ignorance, they are not peculiar. People were not born with the special purpose of making an interpreter uncom-fortable. "There, but for the grace of God, go I," said the prelate as he saw the criminal marched to his doom.

Samuel Taylor Coleridge has explained this to me, who have needed the explanation as much as, and perhaps more than, any:

"If you do not understand a man's ignorance," said Coleridge, "you will remain ignorant of his understanding."

When first I read those words, I confess it sounded to me like a verbal trick. But later the essential truth, the vital importance of it for interpretation, dawned upon me. The interpreter will have no difficulty in translating this aphorism in terms of his own experience. The visitors who come for his services have seldom any expert, or even moderate, knowledge of the things they come to see or to experience. They come frequently with mere idle curiosity, or to kill time, or from boredom. It is for us to understand, and affectionately to weigh, not the ignorance, for that is apparent, but the reasons for the ignorance.

Compared with the usual fate of humans, we who are engaged in preservational work, daily in contact with what we most like and admire, are fortunate indeed. As I write this, I have just returned from a gathering of men and women in the museum and historic-house field. What cheerful, rapt faces! What intensity of interest! What freedom of discussion, where difference of opinion about procedure was taken for granted and met with a smile. Do you really think this is common experience in the workaday world? Are you unaware of the fact that most people often feel that they are traveling the wrong road, and bitterly conclude that it is too late to return to a distant fork?

You cannot change this, but you can understand it; and thus you can account for the poor conditioning of those whom you would delight with an introduction to the treasures in your custody. There is the challenge! to put your visitor in possession of at least one disturbing idea that may grow into a fruitful interest.

Carl Feiss, the city planner, told me that when he was visiting an historic house he observed that a number of people asked the identical question: "Is this place still in the hands of the same family?" There, at least, is a vulnerable spot that most people share in common: the longing for continuity, whether it be of ownership of real estate, of their own family or race, or of the subtler kind that relates the puzzled human to the physical world he sees about him.

Thus, when the interpreter comes to understand the basis of the *ignorance* of his visitor, he is prepared to deal with that auditor's *understanding*. And the understanding is usually ample; only its range is entirely outside, at first glance, what the interpreter knows and feels concerning his wares. When I was guiding hundreds of people through the Castillo in Saint Augustine, it was not difficult to look into the eyes of those who sat before me in the orientation room off the sally port and register the effect I was producing. There was a man who seemed impenetrable until I came to mention the manner in which the great blocks of coquina (shell) rock, quarried on Anastasia Island just across the bay, were used in the construction. Suddenly this man shot a question at me: "How were they *bonded?*" Fortunately, I knew the meaning of the term as he used it, and I was able to explain that the cementing material was at hand for the builders in the form of sharp sand and oyster shells. From that moment he was interested in the fort. He came to me afterward and said, "I want to know more about this. Can you suggest a book about it?" He was a building constructor, and I had touched him where he lived. I had reached his understanding. Now he was on the highroad to history.

Enough of this aspect of love; and now to the love of his subject that the interpreter must possess. "To know a thing," wrote Thomas Carlyle, "what we can call *knowing*, a man must first *love* the thing, sympathize with it: that is, be virtuously related to it." Priceless ingredient, indeed.

I think of a letter written by Frank Pinkley, the first Superintendent of Southwestern Monuments, in the National Park Service. It was not my good fortune to know "Boss" Pinkley, as he was known affectionately, but none other than an extraordinary lover of his work could have left such an impress upon his associates that they cannot mention him without a moistening of eye and a little quaver of voice. Here is Pinkley writing of one of his subordinates who had just left the world:

I was startled the other day to get the news that Park Supervisor Gabriel Sovulewski was no longer on the active list. . . . His park never became commonplace to him . . . he once took me on a geological trip on the floor of the Valley, which wound up at the foot of Capitan.

We sat there three or four minutes; wordless; drinking it all in; and then he said something I have never forgotten: "You can talk all you want to about how this valley was formed, but there is where your science ends and Almighty God begins."

This reverence for what, in our natural world of fitness and beauty, is not factual but of the spirit; for that which is beyond diction; for the very soul of that which the interpreter makes a living and potent reality in a cloudy experience—this reverence is brought into interpretation by love.

"White Mountains" Smith, an old-timer among National Park rangers, expressed his love in an explosive way. Tom Vint tells me that one day he was riding the upper road in Jackson Hole with Smith, when the latter suddenly wheeled his car off into the brushy shoulder, jumped out and drew Tom after him. He swept his arm along the horizon line of the incomparable Tetons and blurted: "By God, Tom, I call that beautiful!" Understand, Smith had seen that jagged horizon line day after day. Far from being jaded, his love saw new beauties every time he looked. Even if his expression was characteristically rugged, you do not need my suggestion that it was as truly reverent as that of Gabriel Sovulewski, companion of "Boss" Pinkley.

Whether the interpreter is placed in primitive surroundings, or at a battlefield, or among the ruins of Pueblo people, or in a house that has sheltered a continuing family for two centuries and a half—all is one. If he is "virtuously related" to it, as Carlyle said, he can people the historic house, the ruins, the battlefield; and in our primeval parks, by the magic of love, he can create the feeling in his hearers that this is the virgin wilderness, with all its associated plant and animal life, which was first glimpsed by the hardy trappers and explorers pushing westward in dangerous but joyous adventure.

In a field where so much specific thinking and action is constantly required, I do not wish to take my readers into a rarefied atmosphere if it can be avoided. But Socrates had a sweep of vision that I am continually finding referable to true interpretation, and I am going to risk a quotation. Socrates said that the prophetess Diotima told him what follows; but Socrates often had tongue in cheek. I think he and Diotima were the same person.

Love is something more than the desire of beauty; it is the instinct of immortality in a mortal creature ... he who has the instinct of true love, and can discern the relations of true beauty in every form, will go on from strength to strength until at last the vision is revealed to him of *a single science*, and he will suddenly perceive a nature of wondrous beauty in the likeness of no human face or form, but absolute, simple, separate and everlasting. ...

Now, I should be somewhat less than honest if I were to pretend that I understood in fullness what Socrates meant by the above. I rather think that Jowett, who so admirably translated the Platonic works, was himself occasionally puzzled. Maybe the Greeks had an intellectual slant that does not quite exist in the modern world. But I have the satisfying feeling that a tremendous truth is here involved.

The word "physis" underwent a number of changes in Greek thought until it came to mean pretty much what we call "nature." I am sure that over the centuries to come, the word "interpretation" will similarly change its meanings to cover a broadened horizon of thinking and to fit new needs and practices.

For the moment, I see in the quoted words of Diotima a curious likeness to the present stage, at least, of our interpretation, when it is good. We start from related or unrelated fact and strive toward a revealing generalization, but finally simplify again in the direction of a statement, or projection of a feeling, that will satisfy any situation because it deals with some element of interest common to all our preservations and common to all visitor experience.

Thus, the six principles with which I began this book may be after all (like the "single science" mentioned by Socrates) a single principle. If this should be so, I feel certain that the single principle must be Love.

CHAPTER XIII

Of Gadgetry

Archimedes:—Give me a fulcrum and I will
move the world. Diogenes:—Will it be better
off in some other place?

WHEN I use the word "gadget" I mean no disrespect. I am
writing this on a gadget; I hope I am not ungrateful, for it
saves me the trouble of pushing, with cramped fingers, a quill pen.
I am sometimes persuaded that the best writing that ever will be
done was in the time of the stylus or the pen-and-foolscap; but if
that be true, it could owe, conceivably, to a decadence in the
writers. Anyhow, since this book is more concerned with the thinking about Interpretation than the excellence of expression, the point
has no large importance.

The fact with which I deal is that, in the field of Interpretation,
the gadget has come to stay, and will be used to a much greater
extent than is now the case. There will never be a device of tele-
communication as satisfactory as the direct contact not merely with
the voice, but with the hand, the eye, the casual and meaningful
ad lib, and with that something which flows out of the very con-
stitution of the individual in his physical self. While I think nobody
disagrees upon this, we all know that there will not be enough of
those individuals to make the direct contact. We shall catch up with
a current requirement only to find ourselves behind again. So,
whether one likes it or not, we are going to have more—and I should
hope, better—mechanical devices aimed at multiplying the interpretive effort.

This means, explicitly, more automatic projection equipment,
more sound installations, more recorders and tapes, more gadgets
to be self-operated by visitors, more motion pictures of fidelity and
professional skill, and so on.

I was in some doubt as to whether a chapter on this subject properly belonged in the kind of book I am writing, because it is apparent that such a mechanical device can never deliver anything better than what some person thought, prepared, spoke or otherwise personally performed. Indeed, it must be, in spite of any electronic perfection of the machine, always a shade toward the worse. The gadget is a willing slave, and repeats even your intake of breath, your *hem*'s and *ha*'s, and your stumbles from the ideal in every way. If I spell *cat* with a *k* on my typewriter, it is not the machine's defect.

Yet, in my long course of study of Interpretation which has taken me so many thousands of miles and into so many and varied preserved areas, I have arrived at some reflections concerning the present use of mechanical devices, and it may be of some little service to announce them here.

1. No device of the kind we here consider is, other things being equal, as desirable as interpretation by direct contact with the person. (I shall not further discuss this, for practically everybody agrees; but it is a good point to start from.)

2. A good device is far better than no contact at all.

3. A good result by device is better than a poor performance by an individual.

4. A poor interpretation by mechanical means is worse than a poor interpretation by personal contact.

5. A poor interpretation by mechanical means is not necessarily better than none at all; it may be worse than none at all, for you may add the same insult to injury as when one imposes upon another person a time-wasting telephone call.

6. No institution should install any mechanical devices until it knows that such gadgets can be adequately, continually, and quickly serviced. No matter how good they may be when they are working properly, they are a source of shame and chagrin, as well as an imposition on the public, when they are allowed to be more than briefly inoperative.

Not long ago I went into a city-owned museum where, in the section devoted to geology, there was a well-selected group of fluorescent minerals in a black-light cabinet. Personally, I delight—

National Park Service, Jack Boucher

A wayside exhibit attracts visitors entering Cades Cove, once an isolated pastoral community, now a part of Great Smoky Mountains National Park. A few families are permitted to remain on the land, grazing their cattle and demonstrating for visitors the old mountain skills.

National Park Service

Old ways of making furniture are demonstrated by a Cades Cove resident.

Cannons are excellent interpretive exhibits, especially if the interpretation includes a simulated firing drill. Fort Point National Historic Site, California.

A school class visiting the Frederick Douglass Home in Washington, D.C., learns about their natural environment through the eyes of a park naturalist.

Uniformed interpreters meet visitors at the Lincoln Memorial, Washington, D.C.

even with a child's delight—in these lovely specimens. But the device was not working. I sought one of the employees, who told me in a courteous but rather weary tone that "it went out of order very easily." His manner clearly suggested to me that it had not been working for some time, and it might be another long time before anything was done about it. So as far as fluorescence was concerned, this device might as well have been stored in the cellar.

I attended a campfire talk in one of our national parks when the visitors, on the first occasion I was present, waited more than half an hour because the voice amplifier was out of order. The folks who attend these campfire talks, I have found, are very patient and grateful for the interpretation offered them; so they were on this occasion. I went to the same place on the following two nights, because each program offered was interesting to me. There was the same mechanical trouble; the same delay. It occurred to me then that actually the amplifier was not needed at all. The circle was small. The amplifier, when it did operate, was badly adjusted and unpleasant. Any one of the speakers I heard (and two of them were uncommonly good, with well-selected slides) could have made himself heard perfectly without resort to a mechanism. We cannot too much stress the fact that any amplification is at best a necessary evil, and that the average speaker with a minimum of proper training can make himself perfectly intelligible without unusual effort where the space is not too great. I shall go no farther into this feature, since there is plenty of literature on the subject.

Finally, in the resort to mechanical devices there is another danger to be avoided. An interpreter confided to me that he looked with pleasure on the coming of such automation because "it will give me more time for research." It should be obvious that this is not the proper purpose. My comment is not to be understood as meaning that the interpreter should not indulge in research if he has the talent for it. He may, on the contrary, very profitably do so. I mean simply that the reason stated is not a good one. In this instance a practical consideration was involved. The current need of the area was for first-hand oral interpretation, not research.

Gadgets do not supplant the personal contact; we accept them as valuable alternatives and supplements.

CHAPTER XIV

The Happy Amateur

In the word amateur there is something lovable, which gives a congenial aspect to the person of whom it is said. With pleasure we say of someone: "he is an amateur," whereby we envision immediately a happy man, a smiling Maecenas, living among beautiful things and appreciating them.

And what, in truth, is an amateur? First, and above all, he is one who finds a consuming interest in studies that are quite aside from his regular work.—Pierre Humbert.

OVER THE YEARS words undergo wear and tear, and some of them emerge the worse for it. When Samuel Johnson wrote his dictionary the word "officious" meant "kindly; helpful." Now if you call a man officious, he is insulted, for you imply that he is an impertinent meddler. When Champlain wrote that Mount Desert Island—now containing Acadia National Park—was "inhabité," he meant that it was a wilderness, exactly the opposite of what we now mean by the word.

But, to me, the saddest fate of any has been suffered by the word "amateur." I am not sure just at what period the fine old noun was perverted for common usage. To most people now it means a dabbler, a bungler, a producer of something inferior. What a pity! for this word once described a person who could not be otherwise than happy, since he was doing something for the love of it; not for material gain, not even for fame or pre-eminence: he or she simply gave the head and heart, and rejoiced. A hobby? No, more than a hobby; though a good hobby has often added years to a life.

No; something of higher meaning, more satisfying to the soul. We shall see.

First, let us consider the dire need for the revival of the amateur spirit. In the past several years there has come into our general magazines a flood of articles dealing with the acute problem of American social life arising from the vast increase of leisure time. This problem engages the thought of the sociologist, the economist and even the psychiatrist. "Are you a week-end neurotic?" is the title of a recent inquiry. The point seemed to be that millions of Americans, having looked forward keenly to the release from their work, find themselves in the clutch of "a deep-seated fear of relax-ation and leisure ... creating feelings of uneasiness, and sometimes of acute illness." The reason is obvious enough: the victims of this week-end moodiness have had no training in the fruitful and pleas-urable use of leisure. But knowing the explanation does not supply the corrective. Unplanned, uninspired free time can be a curse, and we need only to refer to the experience of the Romans to find a practical realization of the fact. The successful Mithridatic wars brought into a conventional hard-working Roman polity a tide of slaves and treasure from the East. There was indeed plenty of leisure as a result. But it ended in donatives (doles) and a social instability that even the ablest autocrats of the Empire were unable to stifle.

Today we are dealing neither with imported slaves nor with the fatness of conquest, but through productive short cuts we reach the same end of more and more leisure.

By contrast, the Greeks of the "golden" period (that of Pericles, let us say) seem to have had a considerable knowledge of the profitable use of their leisure. There were slaves in Athens, too, and a large body besides of people who were neither slave nor franchised. The Greeks of the period certainly had enough faults, but by all accounts they possessed a happy versatility that permitted them to be amateurs of music, of the theatre, of oratory, and of the finesse of logical discussion, and even (if you trust Aristophanes) to have a passion for sitting on juries and enjoy legal hair-splitting. At any rate, you get no idea that the Athenian was bored on his "week end." In a republic that produced such consummate artists and thinkers, it must have been that the people liked it that way. They were a crowd of happy amateurs. Those that could not create, could appreciate and encourage. Happy versatility!

Now, if these observations are substantially correct, they have a vital importance for all those earnest administrators of, and workers in, the national, state and other parks, the publicly and privately owned museums, historic houses—all preserves where some measure of interpretation is involved and practised. For, the thoughtful administrator of such preserves, as well as the interpreter intent upon doing his utmost to realize their greatest possibilities to mind and spirit, is constantly checking and rechecking himself with the blunt and honest question: "Just what is it that I am trying to do? What is the place of this institution, of which I am a part, in the scheme of American life?"

Protection and preservation of the physical memorials of our natural and historic origins is primary, of course. And I suppose a good case could be made for the mere locking-up of our most important treasures—the fragile and the irreplaceable and the "bank deposits" of study in future years—because they are the arks of our covenants and even when not seen are an inspiration through the feeling that they exist and are safe.

But, unfortunately, save in rare instances, this is not at all required. We can *use* these precious resources, so long as we do not *use them up*. Put it this way: We should not dissipate our capital, but we should zealously dispense the interest.

Ah, but how? That is what the interpreter wants to know. A good generalization would be: We maintain these preserves so that all the people will have access to the source material of our natural and historic origins, besides having the relaxation and novelty of coming into a world apart from their daily round, and into the presence of beauty, art, the significant moment and the stirring event. But how is this laudable purpose to be translated into a continuing interest that does not end, but really begins, when our visitor has left the park, the museum, or the historic place?

Even if it were desirable—and it is not—to create a nation of accomplished specialists through visits to such places, the interpreter knows that this is impossible. The take-home acquisition of direct education derived by the visitor is pitifully small, for he has not come to be educated. He has come to see, to sample, to try something new. Is Grand Canyon really as wonderful as Joe Smith told me? He has heard that "everybody ought to visit" Fort Laramie, or the Vanderbilt Mansion, or Monticello. "All right; I am here. Show me."

The visitor doesn't know it, but he has walked into a delightful trap. From his very curiosity and vagueness of purpose, he has given the interpreter a chance. What chance? Well, certainly not to send him away with a packet of specific information. If he should happen to be at Fort Laramie, he will not remember whether a certain unfortunate commander's name was Fetterman, or Winckelman, or Peabody, or what year the fort was established. No; the opportunity is to make a happy amateur of him by thrilling him with the story of the great western trek of the American; the plodding of the hobnailed boots over the Oregon Trail toward the sunset; the conquest of the West; the flowering of the Territories. The tale of Laramie is a significant part, but the whole picture is the one that may engage your visitor in a love that will take care of his leisure time.

We do have such happy amateurs already; many and many of them; but far, far from enough for our national welfare. Have you heard of the groups called "The Westerners"? There are your happy amateurs! There may be qualified historians among them, but most are men of many trades who get together, not merely to toss a glass and eat a snack, but to match minds in the fascinating historical quest of which they are all lovers. So it is with the many who gather at what are called the "Civil War Round Tables." If you have ever attended one of these meetings, you could never suppose any one of the amateurs of our domestic war would be at a loss to employ his leisure time with delight. There may be, for all I know, neurotics among them, but the neurosis does not arise for such a reason.

And somehow this reminds me that one does not need the background of a formal education to become an amateur of either art or science. The case of Marc Navarrete and his father, Fred, who live on a ranch near Naco, Arizona, is a cheerful instance of this fact. Of these two men, Dr. Emil W. Haury, of the University of Arizona, has written: "The exemplary attitude and the alertness of the Navarretes shine as a beacon on the relationship between the interested amateur and the specialist. It is my sincere hope that the vital part these men have played in adding to a clearer understanding of Early Man in the Southwest will be a lasting satisfaction to them."

Fred and Marc Navarrete had for some fifteen years been watching an arroyo eroded by Greenbush Creek, as it widened and deepened. I do not know how the Navarretes became interested in archeology. But it certainly could have been due to a visit to one of the National Park Service archeological areas in the Southwest. At all events, Marc Navarrete brought word to the Arizona State Museum in September, 1951, of his discovery of two large projectile points in close association with mammoth bones. Being a true amateur, he knew the importance of what he had found. Likewise, being a true amateur, he realized that further exploration was for the specialists. The subsequent digging on Greenbush Creek and the finding of eight projectile points clearly indicating a prehistoric "kill" and butchering at least ten thousand years ago was, as Emil Haury says, "a triumph of the amateur spirit." Can you suppose the Navarretes become restless and ill because they find their week ends a bore?

I have indicated, early in this chapter, a difference between the hobbyist and the amateur. I have no sneers against hobbies. The hobbyist may, and frequently does, develop into a fine amateur. But I think, generally speaking, the man with a hobby is interested in *things,* while the amateur is engaged primarily with *ideas* or *culture.* The collection of coins, for example, is a hobby, and a worthy one. But when you have assembled large American pennies of every date and mint, that job is complete. If you are not tired of it, you start again with another kind of coin.

But suppose you dabble in antique coins, Greek or Roman. Long before your accumulation embarrasses your finances, you find yourself, through these coins, becoming acquainted with the social and economic life of these nations of the past. I am not a numismatist; but when I see on a Roman coin the word *Annona*

Visitors in Mesa Verde National Park investigate at close range the multi-storied Indian cliff dwelling preserved there.

Participation is a valuable ingredient of interpretation. Visitors get wet and "mucky" in a swamp tromp in Everglades National Park.

Other Everglades visitors have a close look at wildlife on an interpretive tram ride through the Shark Valley.

Ranger with children at Cathedral Grove in Muir Woods in northern California.

or the word *Liberalitas* I know that I am being told a story of the gradual bankruptcy of the Empire, and I can see in an adulterated "silver" coin of Gallienus the end of that economic dance when the emperors had no more dole-money to quiet the mobs.

With Greek coins it is the same. You begin to understand why the "owl" of Athens was eagerly sought by the other States that had tinkered with their currency. It was "good" money; even in the silliest political moments of the Athenians, they avoided debasing the bird of Minerva. Pereskius, one of the learned men of the late Renaissance, used ancient coins to study ancient history; and Pereskius was not a professional but an amateur historian.

The opportunities arising to create happy amateurs seem to me to be almost innumerable in the natural and scientific areas of the national and state and municipal parks. Already we have many hundreds of thousands of people who delight in birds, in rocks and minerals, in flowers and trees, even in meteorology, with no intention whatever of making a profession of such interests.

Recently there was a news dispatch, widely printed, originating in Ottawa, Canada:

WHOOPING CRANES HAVE NOT ARRIVED

You might think, in the midst of whirling world politics, that nobody would care a whoop whether the whooping cranes had arrived anywhere, or even that they had left anywhere. But news agencies do not squander lineage. And, indeed, that bit of news came close to many people who, to be sure, will never see a whooping crane, but who are amateurs of wildlife in the noblest possible way. Because wildlife is part of our precious record of evolution, and because, as Professor J. Arthur Thompson said, "these humbler creatures are wrapped up in the bundle of life with ourselves," not a single species should be permitted to perish—at least not because of any fault of ours.

The growth of interest in rocks and minerals, especially on the part of children, has in the past quarter century been simply astounding. It continues at a rapid rate, and not long ago the manufacturer of a breakfast cereal tried the experiment of enclosing a mineral specimen in each package, with the promise of supplying a number of others. The samples were insignificant in size, and needed some reference to make them important; yet it was a strangely humane and intelligent device to spring from modern advertising.

Here, again, I suggest the difference between the mere desire to make a collection of something (a good thing in its way) and the amateur spirit that deals with larger and more satisfying concepts. It is quite possible to assemble a cabinet of very fine crystals—of quartz, tourmalines, garnets, and the like—and never give much thought to the mystery of our inorganic partners of life. It is when you hold even an unshowy bit of rock in hand and consider that this sort of thing made our own life possible by being broken down into soil by tiny plants, by sun and snow and other agencies; when you sit upon a strayed boulder left by glaciation, and consider the time when plants and wildlife, and perhaps even Man in our own country, had to move southward away from an increasing frigidity he could not understand; when rocks and minerals begin to add up to a big sum in our own frail origins—then you are on the way toward the status of a happy amateur. If you have ever seen a bus load of "rock-hounds" clambering over some old quarry or mine dump, or attended one of their meetings when they swapped specimens and experiences, you would conclude that at least some part of our population does not become neurotic because it cannot measure up to its holiday spell.

Let us look the facts in the eye: There is at the moment more leisure time than the majority of people seem to be able to convert to the enrichment of mind and spirit. There will be more leisure time, apparently, in days to come. The formal institutions of education direct little or no effort to fill this void. I am not saying that they should. Perhaps it is indeed their business to produce effective specialists, intelligent producers of goods or means. I am sure you would annoy the ordinary educator if you suggested that he install a course in the highest uses of leisure time.

As for what is called "adult education," this seems to tend, whatever its worth, in the same direction. It fills crevices that were left through misfortune, lack of opportunity, lethargy or slow development; but the end seems to be about the same: to make a better worker or specialist. And you still have the week end with you.

It seems to me that in this circumstance the great hope for aiding people in the direction of a happy and fruitful use of leisure is to be found in the national parks, the state and local parks, the museums and other cultural preserves. And, by the same token, I think that here lies the greatest challenge to the interpreter who works in this field: what to do; what to say; how to point the way; how to connect the visitor's own life with something, even one thing, among all the custodial treasures; how finally to elicit from the aimless visitor the specific thought: "This is something I believe I could get interested in." Well, there lies an ideal to work for. But of one thing I am sure: it cannot be done merely by displaying wares, nor by imparting mere facts. The thing is a thing of the spirit; and, to indulge in a rash paraphrase, it must be directed in spirit and in truth.

As to the "happy amateur," I am aware that I have exaggerated a little. We cannot at best do quite that for everybody. I say the ideal is good, though. And let us try to redeem that fine word amateur from its stained condition: shine it up and use it wealthily.

Remember, Benjamin Franklin was an amateur. He stood before kings, he was a member of scientific societies, he was inventor, he was diplomat, he was man of politics and letters; but when he wrote his will, he began, "I, Benjamin Franklin, printer...."

Printing was Franklin's craft; in the other fields he regarded himself as a happy amateur. The other accomplishments richly engaged his leisure time.

CHAPTER XV

Vistas of Beauty

> Truth, and goodness, and beauty, are but different faces of the same All. Beauty in nature is not ultimate. It is the herald of inward and eternal beauty . . . it must stand as a part and not yet as the last or highest expression of the final cause of Nature.—Ralph Waldo Emerson.

IN FEBRUARY, 1965, President Johnson sent to the Congress of the United States a message "On the Natural Beauty of Our Country." It was a state paper probably unique in the history of government. Can anyone recall a similar instance when a nation's leader has proclaimed the vital importance of Beauty in human welfare and moved to salvage what remains of the lovely heritage that a thrusting, feverish, ruthless technology has dilapidated to the point of ugliness? This is a Great Chart. And the time to preserve, to repair, to cease being a nation of prosperous slovens, is now.

The German poet Goethe said, "We should do our utmost to encourage the Beautiful, for the Useful encourages itself." Indeed, utility needs nothing other than its physical materials to work upon. We need not quarrel with that. And it was inevitable that the primeval landscape of America would be vastly altered; that the rich resources would be eagerly tapped and exploited; that rivers should be harnessed, prairies plowed, that roads should scar the land surface, that virgin forests should fall. Nor could it be expected that, except for a few souls gifted with insight, a people aiming at a fuller and more comfortable existence would exercise a philosophic restraint. There is no deep villain in this very human drama. There is only a saddening imbalance that was bound to ensue. Man does not live by bread and gadgets alone. Take Beauty out of his life: a googol of dollars and a Lucullan luxury will not fill the void.

The imbalance is here. It is shockingly manifest. Because of an erupting population, we see the places of natural beauty retreating from the millions as fast as they seek and move toward them; urban slums where people feebly degenerate; roadways lined with the horrible corpses of junked automobiles and with the vulgarities of clamoring commerce; our air polluted with fumes and our rivers and lakes and estuaries so laden with filth and chemicals that fish are killed and humans endangered. The whole drab picture is outlined in President Johnson's message, in measured terms.

Will the President's appeal be effective? There are already signs that it will. The regeneration will take time. Nature repairs ills of the abused human body by slow processes; ills of the spirit even more slowly. There are signs of awakening on all political levels. But it is a warning that must come into the realization of every citizen. Josiah Royce said that the philosopher Immanuel Kant "had small interest in noble sentiments, but very great natural respect for large and connected personal and social undertakings, when guided by ideas." The point is timely. The appeal for the restoration of Beauty to her rightful eminence cannot remain merely a "noble sentiment." It needs action, and not merely in the field of legislation; it must enter the understanding of all of us.

II

But the message to the Congress has far wider significance than appears upon its surface, or in its words. What *is* Natural Beauty? What, indeed, is *Beauty*?

The wisest philosophers have failed to define or to explain this human emotion to which, in our English language, is given the name of Beauty. There is an equivalent word in every language. Paul Shorey, reflecting his study of Plato, said that feeling for beauty is "a touch of noble unrest; the reaching for something of finer quality than the dailiness of life." The love of beauty, he added, becomes the guide toward the perception of the Good and the True. Vague as this may seem, at first glance, it will serve as the path along which our quest for understanding must go. Surely we deal with an essence that is beyond our powers of expression. But we can, and we do, feel its reality.

In the realm of natural beauty, apprehended through the sense of sight mainly, but also by the other organs, we are first overwhelmed by the more spectacular forms. "Breath-taking" is a hackneyed expression; yet it is accurate. The pulse reflects the surge. Beyond that impact, we can come to understand that what we have sensed is only a gorgeous greeting. Behind that curtain lies an infinite world of detailed beauties. As we develop realization of those composing elements, we know that there can be nothing ugly in nature. Nothing. The seeming exceptions are simply facets of beauty we have not yet grasped.

Sometimes we think, in our egotism, that nature has provided these beauties as a special act on our behalf. If I may be allowed a harmless bit of fantasy, I shall imagine a conversation you might have with Nature on this point. After hearing you patiently on the subject of Beauty, Nature would perhaps say something like this:

"I see the source of your error. It derives from your very limited knowledge. You are thinking that I have a Department of Beauty—that I deal with beauty as one of my activities. Really, I do not *intend* beauty. I *am* beauty. I am beauty and many other things, such as you are trying to express by your abstractions like Order, Harmony, Truth, Love. What you see in my scenic manifestations is the glamour behind which lies an Absolute Beauty of which I myself am an expressive part. You do not understand? Naturally it is difficult. But you are trying: I do like *that* in you, little man."

No, we can only shadowly comprehend, and perhaps the mystery will always tantalize us. But, fortunately for our spiritual welfare, we live with the Fact. And this fact is, that in the presence of unsullied, unexploited "raw" nature, we are lifted to a height beyond ourselves. Our first physical contact with Yosemite, with the Tetons, the redwood groves, the Alps, the falls of the Iguazu—with such spectacles wherever they exist—leaves us with an indelible coloring such as has not dominated our thoughts and feelings before. That is the Fact. The metaphysical reasoning about it is more engaging than important. We grow in dimension and capacity. Not only that. We become more sensitive to the opposite of Beauty: ugliness, defacement, disharmony.

Although the purely aesthetic aspect of this Absolute Beauty is but the prologue to a whole, its importance must not be minimized. It is as basic as the letters of the alphabet. Without those letters there are no words; and without words no communication.

III

While our people have been remiss in the sacrifice of beauty to utility, and the time has come to take account of stock, as the President asked, there is still much to our credit. In a period of explosive growth such as few nations have known, possessors of a technological skill that has finally become more than a little frightening, we have yet managed to set aside and wisely to administer a system of National Parks that evokes the admiration of the world. It is true that we had rare advantages, and time was on our side. But it is also true that we had from our earliest days a large and articulate group of forward-thinking men and women alive to the need for preserving the treasures of our culture and the integrity of our inheritance before, as in other lands, it was too late. So that, as the case stands, it is not so much that we have been unmindful of spiritual and moral values: we have not been sufficiently alert to the somber truth that "the Useful encourages itself," while the preservation and affirmation of Beauty needs a constant renewal of faith and the watchful devotion of a shepherd. Nor can our preserved places of natural beauty and memorials of the historic past prosper and remain inspirational if they become islands in an environment of sanctioned ugliness. This is a very nullification of our reverence for beauty. To paraphrase Lincoln: our cultural and spiritual aspirations must shrivel in a world half beautiful, half loathsome. We shall not expect the impossible. But there must be in our mechanized and controlled ecology, while we confess that we have violated much natural beauty physically, and defend it as unavoidable, a manifestation that we still retain the spirit, and show it in our national housekeeping. That is where we have failed.

IV

As I have said, this message is something not merely for legislation, though that is imperatively desirable, but for all of us to meditate. What are its implications, for example, in the work of the

National Park System, where so much natural beauty, majestic and awe-inspiring, and so many less obvious beauties, even hidden ones, are the current stock-in-trade? The very business of the National Park Service is the custodianship and interpretation of Beauty. How could it be otherwise? The interpreter, whether naturalist or ranger or historian or mechanic, is a middleman of this precious cultural wealth.

Viewed as an absolute, Beauty has numberless aspects. For the purpose of the interpreter, I think we need be directly concerned with but four:

1. The park visitor's sensuous contact with scenic or landscape beauty—with "wildness."

2. The beauty of the Adventure of the Mind: the revelation of the Order of Nature.

3. The beauty of the Artifact: Man's aspiration to create beautiful things.

4. The beauty of human conduct, or behavior, of which Man has shown himself capable.

(a)

It is axiomatic that natural beauty, as perceived by the organs of sense, needs no interpretation: it interprets itself. Here the interpreter acts only as a scout and a guide. He leads his groups to the most alluring scenes he has discovered, and is silent. Would you varnish the orchid? He refrains even from using the word "beauty." To suggest that his visitors are to consider either the scene or the song of the hermit thrush as beautiful is even an affront. They *know*. In this aspect Beauty is a precious personal possession. It is the individual's shock, *his* apprehension, *his* discovery: and what he discovers is more than what he sees or hears. He has discovered something of himself, hitherto unrealized. No; we do not interpret that aspect of beauty. It is an exhibit.

(b)

Exactly at this point is where the office of the interpreter begins. There is a concealed beauty that does not appear to the senses. Indeed, this aspect takes two forms. It involves a revelation of the natural beauty we think of as Order—nature at work—and the beauty of that development of the human mind which makes it possible for Man partly to understand it. What are the forces that created what one sees, and feels, as beautiful?

In this book my aim has been, besides giving a working definition of Interpretation, to lay down a set of principles that should be in the mind of the interpreter. As to my definition, I have never been wholly happy, but nobody has seemed to offer a better one, so I rest with it. But, as to the face-to-face communication which the field interpreter is privileged to have with the millions who come to our parks, I have come to feel that I missed something—a factor of extreme importance.

Whether we call it so or not, the interpreter is engaged in a kind of education. It is not the classroom kind. It is, if you will, a proffer of teaching; but it is not the professorial sort. It aims not to *do something* to the listener, but *to provoke the listener to do something to himself*. It is a delicate job, requiring the greatest discretion. The man on holiday does not wish to be lectured; he did not come to a park to be educated. Even the most discerning, and therefore, successful, interpreter must feel conscious of the fact that the materials upon which he works are by their very nature—what shall I say? not *cold*, but certainly *cool*. We appeal to the head, to the mind.

Can we not infuse into this worthy activity an appeal to the heart: to attain something of that impact which nature does so easily and implicitly by presenting the beautiful landscape? Erosion and mountain building, the adaptation of life to its environment, the grand and vital organic community of which man is only a species, however a dominant one—all these entertaining revelations of man's place in nature are at last a presentation of an aspect of the Beautiful. If the interpreter feels this to be so, he can project that feeling. Not by a preachment about it. Heavens, no. It is something to be felt, not analyzed. If deeply felt, it can be communicated.

The scenes upon which you have looked, and the natural sounds you have heard, you regard as Beauty. How did it all come about? By a process that science aims to know more and more about; but whatever we may discover, one thing is sure about that process—it is even more beautiful than that that the eye or ear perceives. This is an appeal to the heart, the soul, or whatever you wish to call it, which constantly yearns to be satisfied. It is warmth. Added to understanding, it is the objective of interpretation.

A great American chemist, Robert S. Mulliken, recently received a Nobel prize. This man once wrote something that has deeply affected my thinking about this world of natural beauties: "The scientist must develop enormous tolerance in seeking for ideas which *may please nature*, and enormous patience, self-restraint and humility when his ideas over and over again are rejected by nature before he arrives at one to *please her*. When the scientist does finally find such an idea, there is something very intimate in his feeling of communion with nature [The italics are mine]."

When the non-scientist understands what Mulliken meant when he talked of "pleasing nature" he will be on his way to understanding the scientific mind. He will realize what the pure scientist means when he talks of a "beautiful equation"—the statement of an idea in artistic form with an economy of means. We "please nature" when we search for, find, and *feel* Beauty. It is as simple as that, yet it is not simply attained and maintained in a world where the marketplace dominates.

(c)

When we come to the beauty of the artifact—man's inspiration to produce with his own hands something of the quality that he has observed in his natural surroundings—we are in a complex and baffling domain. Much we must guess. A paleolithic artist incised on the wall of a cave at Altamira the figure of a running deer. The draftsmanship, resulting from the acute observation of this prehistoric man, is by modern standards a beautiful thing. But did he intend beauty, or was it a propitiation of the spirit of the chase—a magical device to procure meat, and therefore a matter of utility? We cannot know: surely there is no harm in concluding that it could have been both. I have held in my hand the bowl of a ceremonial pipe, made of the red Catlinite claystone that came from southwestern Minnesota, but taken from a mound in northern

Mississippi, the work of one of our prehistoric Indian artists. It is the figure of a man sitting and thinking—a forerunner of the famous Rodin sculpture, and not a whit less impressive. Did this early artist intend beauty? I think he did; though there may have been religious significance.

But clearly we are here in a region of taste, tradition, changing standards of judgment. The interpreter of the story of the artifact is not dealing with beauty as such, but with man's attitude toward beauty; and this can be made warmly appealing, for it is an appeal to the heart even more than to the mind. The standards of judgment in architecture change. The filigree gingerbread of the Victorian period is today a matter of mild amusement. Structures that were considered beautiful in their time cause pained surprise now. Yet, worldwide, there are not many people who do not thrill at the classic beauty of the Parthenon, the Maison Carré at Nîmes, or the Lincoln Memorial in Washington. And all of us are sensitive to harmony of structure and environment. The humble adobe dwelling arising from our southwestern desert, created from the desert soil itself, and roofed with rush or with tiles shaped on the thigh of the builder, violates no principle of art. The most expensive structure, of architectural merit in itself, but alien to its environment, may be an excrescence—almost an ugliness. Hence the fine current effort around Washington to procure scenic easements. The objection is not so much to the artifacts themselves: in relation to the greater natural beauty they may be in the wrong place.

One could go on endlessly in a discussion of the opportunity for the interpretation of man's aspiration to produce beautiful objects. More to the point at the moment is the effort to restore some of the natural beauty we have blighted, and to make resurgent an innate delight in the beauty of our environment: the aim of the program of beautification to which the wife of the President has given her enthusiasm and the prestige of her position.

As the interpreter, in or out of the National Park Service, is not needed to define or explain scenic beauty, neither does its opposite require interpretation. When Alice was in Wonderland the Mock Turtle told her that he went to school with an old turtle who taught Uglification.

"I never heard of 'Uglification,' " Alice ventured to say. The Gryphon lifted up both its paws in surprise.

"Never heard of uglifying," it exclaimed. "You know what to beautify is, I suppose?"

"Yes," said Alice, doubtfully. "It means to make anything prettier."

"Well, then," the Gryphon went on, "if you don't know what to uglify is, you *are* a simpleton."

Well we know what Ugliness is, and the processes that create it. In the haste to gain material welfare we have forgotten, or chosen to forget; and the bill has now come due. To live willingly in tawdry surroundings is to become numb to their baleful influence upon us; they tend to seem as inevitable as climate. It is not so. It is already proved, in city, state, county, and town, that the feeling for beauty can be dramatized and renewed by *beautifying*. The start has been made.

What interpreters can do is to communicate, from their own conviction, *by indirection but with warmth*, this appeal to an always receptive human heart.

(d)

In the interpretation of the beauty of conduct of which the human being is capable, we come under the leering squint of the pessimist. We read in Emerson that "the beauty of nature must always seem unreal and mocking, until the landscape has human figures that are as good as itself."

"Perhaps," replies the cynic, "but tell me just when that will be."

We do not have to go back to antiquity—to Socrates, Jesus, or the Roman general Regulus, for the answer to that. It is here and now, just as it was yesterday and the day before. The National Park System includes scores of historic memorials, the truest interpretation of which is the evidence that our country has possessed men and women of great moral beauty. And for each one of those a myriad of the humbler unknowns has lived and passed. The birthplace of Washington; the several areas that keep in memory the greatheartedness of Lincoln; the house at Appomattox where Grant and Lee revealed beautiful magnanimity on the one side and a nobility in the acceptance of defeat on the other; the farmer soldiers at the bridge in Concord; an ample preservation of the Civil War battlefields—what are all these but the testimonials that man does transcend his animal boundary?

Recently in Vietnam, a soldier threw himself upon a hand grenade, saving the lives of his comrades. War is a terrible thing; the hope of mankind is that it will cease to be; yet it cannot be denied that out of its shambles have emerged valor and fortitude and self-sacrifice on the part of individual man and woman. William James, the Harvard philosopher, had this undeniable truth in mind when he wrote his "Moral Equivalent for War"—an attempt to find some other agent in life that would perform the same service to human character. That he failed is less important than that he showed his own beauty of conduct in the failure.

The interpreter in a monument or battlefield of war may thrill his hearer with the account of the mass action; the losses and gains in a swaying conflict; the skill of leadership. This can be made dramatic stuff, exciting the imagination, a capsuled fragment of the national past that must not be forgotten. But these things are an appeal to the mind, to logic and imagination. The appeal to the heart is the story of how in such tragic environment the human being finds the path to beauty of behavior.

V

The appeal for a renaissance of the appreciation of Beauty—in the abstract and in its particular aspects—must not be allowed to falter. It is vital to our moral growth. It is a program of education. Perhaps it is truer to say that it is a program of re-education, for we have always known, in our innermost recesses, our dependence upon Beauty for the courage to face the problems of life. We have let ourselves forget. It is the duty of the interpreter to jog our memories.

Index